Conte.

Series Foreword

The Zeuthen Lectures offer a forum for leading scholars to develop and synthesize novel results in theoretical and applied economics. They aim to present advances in knowledge in a form accessible to a wide audience of economists and advanced students of economics. The choice of topics will range from abstract theorizing to economic history. Regardless of the topic, the emphasis in the lecture series will be on originality and relevance. The Zeuthen Lectures are organized by the Institute of Economics, University of Copenhagen.

The lecture series is named after Frederik Zeuthen, a former professor at the Institute of Economics.

Karl Gunnar Persson

Foreword

At least since Adam Smith wrote about compensating wage differentials, economists have been interested in understanding why workers are paid differently. A main theory in this area takes the view that wage differentials are consequences of the productive capability incorporated in the workers and that interest centers on the decision to invest in productive capability or human capital. However, plain inspection and the evidence from empirical research suggest that this is not enough to explain wage dispersion. *(similar workers (same productive capability/HK) are paid differently).*

Another topic, which is as old as the profession, is the attempt to understand unemployment. The major theory in this area is job search theory, whereby workers are assumed to face different options in the labor market. A natural question in this context is why similar workers should receive offers that differ with respect to wage rates, as is the assumption in the partial job search models.

This book is about the recent attempts to explain both transitions in the labor market and the distribution of wages in the labor market in a coherent way. The point of departure is the "Burdett-Mortensen model." In this general equilibrium model of the labor market, ex ante identical workers move between unemployment and ex ante identical firms, which pay different wage rates. The arrival of the Burdett-Mortensen model triggered a considerable and rapidly expanding literature. There are both empirical contributions, which attempt to estimate the parameters of the model, and theoretical contributions, which attempt to extend the basic model in order to improve the ability of the model to predict different phenomena in the labor market.

The book offers an introduction to the basic model, whereby both transition rates and wage distributions are obtained as endogenous entities. The extensions of the basic model are reviewed, especially models that allow for differences in firm productivity and different types of contracts between employers and employees. In addition it is shown how other theories of wage determination can be incorporated into this framework, such that it is possible to understand empirical phenomena, which so far have been difficult to explain.

However, the book is not only a theoretical exercise. It also presents evidence of the relevance of existing empirical literature to wage formation. Furthermore, it contributes to the empirical literature by presenting calculations of empirical counterparts to the various theoretical concepts. The data source is the Integrated Database for Labor Market Research (IDA), the Danish matched employer-employee research database.

The book is an authoritative review of the fascinating line of thought, which makes it possible to make a complete characterization of important aspects of the labor market in a general equilibrium model described by very few parameters. Moreover, empirical-oriented researchers, who question the usefulness of estimating highly structural models, have found the basic line of thought relevant with respect to understanding empirical phenomena on the labor market.

Throughout the book Dale Mortensen emphasizes how wage formation in relation to the transition processes on the labor market can be viewed in game theory context. Frederik Zeuthen's solution concept of wage bargaining between employers and employees was the outcome of a process (the Zeuthen-Nash-Harsanyi solution, as it is sometimes called), and this volume thus falls very neatly into the Zeuthen Lecture Book Series.

Karsten Albæk

Preface

The book began as a record of my Zeuthen Lectures by the same title delivered at the University of Copenhagen in November 2000. Parts of the penultimate version were presented as a MacIntosh Lecture at Queens University in March 2002 and as a Schumpeter Lecture Series at Humboldt University in June 2002. The material is also familiar to the students in recent presentations of my course in graduate labor economics.

The empirical content of the book is based on joint research with B. J. Christensen, Rasmus Lentz, George Neumann, and Axel Werwatz. That project started subsequent to my 1998 research leave at the Centre for Labour Market and Social Research (CLS) in Aarhus, Denmark, where I was introduced to the Danish matched employer-worker data. I wish to thank my old friends and colleagues, Niels Westergaard-Nielsen and Henning Bunzel, who as CLS research directors supported and encouraged both the project and the book. My editor, Kathy Caruso, also deserves my gratitude.

I am particularly grateful to those individuals who read all or parts of the book and provided specific comments and corrections. These include Gadi Barlevy, Loujia Hu, Rasmus Lentz, George Neumann, Kenneth Burdett, Robert Shimer, Karsten Albæk, and Hugo Nopo. Research support from the National Science Foundation, the Danish National Research Foundation, and Northwestern University is also acknowledged.

Introduction

Both "good" and "bad" jobs coexist. In a U.S. context, a good job pays well, provides for a paid vacation, and offers health insurance and other related benefits. Of course, occupations that require more skill have a larger fraction of better jobs in all of these senses. Still, observably identical workers are found in both good and bad jobs in close proximity at the same time. These observations motivate the question addressed in these lectures: Why are similar workers paid differently?

In a hypothetical perfectly competitive market, each worker chooses employment that offers the maximal utility across all possible job opportunities. In this environment, wage differences across workers reflect only variation in individual worker ability and/or differences in the nonpecuniary attributes of the jobs held. Although hundreds if not thousands of empirical studies that estimate so-called human capital wage equations verify that worker characteristics that one could view as indicators of labor productivity are positively related to wages earned, the theory is woefully incomplete in its explanatory power. Observable worker characteristics that are supposed to account for productivity differences typically explain no more than 30 percent of the variation in compensation across workers in these studies. In what follows, I refer to the residual, the 70 percent of the variation that remains unexplained by worker characteristics, as wage dispersion.

There are numerous reasons for interest in a convincing theory of wage dispersion. First, wage inequality is a major source of household inequality in wealth and consumption. Labor income accounts for about two-thirds of aggregate income and a much larger share of the income of most households. Indeed, the households that earn the lowest wages are typically among the poorest in any country. Furthermore, real earnings of low-wage earners have actually fallen in the last twenty years in the United States while high-wage workers have experienced significant *[handwritten margin notes: Inequality has risen / Growth in wage dispersion; US: Real earnings ↓ poor ↓ and ↑ for rich (holding worker characteristics constant); firm size]*

growth in earnings. Growth in wage dispersion is a major contributor to the recent increase in U.S. wage differences across workers holding worker characteristics constant.[1] Second, the existence of differences in wages not accounted for by differences in ability raises questions about economic efficiency. For example, if the observed wage dispersion reflects differences in the marginal productivity of labor across employers rather than workers, then total output can be increased by encouraging the reallocation of workers from the lesser to the more productive activities. Finally, large wage differences across employers suggest the existence of significant match rents. How these are allocated between worker and employer can also affect the efficiency of the process by which workers are allocated to jobs. Hence, anyone interested in either efficiency or equity in the labor market needs to understand wage dispersion.

As suggested by the fact that standard wage equations explain a relatively small fraction of the variation in wages across individuals, documenting the existence of wage dispersion is a no-brainer. This fact should have long ago led labor economists to question the efficacy of the standard competitive model as the accepted mechanism of wage determination. However, many argue that the 70 percent of log wage variation is not explained by observed ability differences that can be accounted for by unobservables. Is it possible that the unexplained variation simply represents relevant unobserved worker characteristics?

There are systematic regularities in wage differentials supporting the alternative proposition that differences in pay policy exist across firms. This evidence suggests that different employers do pay similar workers differently. For example, the empirical literature on wage determination finds a positive association between wages paid and firm size. Large and persistent inter-industry wage differentials are also well documented. Krueger and Summers (1988) established that wage premiums in specific industries are similar across time periods and countries. Empirical studies on the firm size differential for the United States and other countries include Brown and Medoff (1989) and Oi and Idson (1999). According to Davis and Haltiwager (1996), increases in the magnitude of size effects have contributed significantly to dispersion in average wages paid across manufacturing establishment in the United States. Because all of these authors control for observable worker characteristics, the size and industry differentials reflect wage dispersion as defined earlier. Still, these measured differentials could be the consequence of correlations between unobserved worker ability and job attribute differences and the size and industry category of the employing firms.

Explanations for industry and size differentials fall, then, into two general categories. The differences can arise because different firms have different wage policies and/or because high paying firms employ workers who are more productive for reasons that are not observed in the data. In the literature on industry differentials, Krueger and Summers (1988) emphasize the former explanation while Murphy and Topel (1990) argue that unmeasured differences in individual ability tell the principal story. Although work by Dickens and Katz (1987) and Gibbons and Katz (1992) attempt to resolve the debate, their efforts were hampered by a lack of appropriate data.

Indeed, since the differential wage policy hypothesis implies the existence of a firm fixed effect in the wage equation and the unobserved ability argument suggests that one should include a worker fixed effect, matched panel data on individual workers and their employers is required to decide the empirical debate. Data of this kind has only recently become available. In their pathbreaking work analyzing data from both France and the state of Washington (United States), Abowd, Kramarz, and Margolis (1999), Abowd, Finer, and Kramarz (1999), and Abowd and Kramarz (2000a,b) have decomposed industry and size differentials into average employer and worker components.[2] They find that the two effects are roughly equally important in explaining inter-industry differences in both the state of Washington and in France while the average employer effect can explain over 70 percent of the size differential in both cases. These results provide ample evidence for the importance of wage policy as well as unobserved ability differences as sources of inter-industry and firm-size wage differentials.

What is the explanation for differences in worker pay policy? It seems clear that some form of imperfect competition is necessary. The notion of a pay policy presumes that employers have market power in the sense that each can set its own wage. This power is not monopsony in the literal sense of a "single buyer" of labor services but rather in the sense that each firm faces an upward sloping supply curve given the wages paid by competitors.[3] Interestingly, Samuelson (1951, 554) sketched the essential elements of a pay policy theory in his economic principles text:[4]

The fact that a firm of any size must have a wage policy is additional evidence of labor market imperfections. In a perfectly competitive market a firm need not make decisions on its pay schedules; instead it would turn to the morning newspaper to learn what its wage policy would have to be. Any firm, by raising wages ever so little, could get all the extra help it wanted. If, on the other hand, it cut the wage ever so little, it would find no labor to hire at all.

But just because competition is not 100 percent perfect does not mean that it must be zero. The world is a blend of (1) competition and (2) some degree of monopoly power over the wage to be paid. A firm that tries to set its wage too low will soon learn this. At first nothing much need happen; but eventually it will find its workers quitting a little more rapidly than would otherwise be the case. Recruitment of new people of the same quality will get harder and harder, and slackening off in the performance and productivity of those who remain on the job will become noticeable.

Availability of labor supply does, therefore, affects the wage you set under realistic conditions of imperfect competition. If you are a very small firm you may even bargain and haggle with prospective workers so as to not pay more than you have to. But if you are of any size at all, you will name a wage for each type of job, then decide how many of the applicants will be taken on.

Why is the labor supply curve faced by an individual employer less than infinitely elastic? One of my own teachers, Martin Bronfenbrenner (1956, 577–578), makes explicit the argument hinted at in Samuelson's words:

The typical employer in an unorganized labor market is by no means a pure competitor facing market wages which he cannot alter. The mobility of the labor force, even between firms located close together, is low by reason of the inability of workers to wait for employment or risk unemployment, plus the inadequacy of the information usually available to them regarding alternative employment opportunities. This low mobility permits each to set his own rates and form his own labour market within limits which are sometimes quite wide. In the technical jargon of economic theory, the typical employer in an unorganized labor market has some degree of monopsony power and can set his own wage policy.

It is not that theorists have been totally silent on the issue of monopsonistic competition in the labor market. Phelps (1970) and Mortensen (1970) suggested a theoretical approach to the problem some time ago. They argue that employers face a less than perfectly elastic labor supply because unemployed applicants are willing to accept low wage offers and cannot instantaneously move to higher paying employers as Bronfenbrenner points out. In this environment, a high-paying employer profits by attracting and retaining a larger labor force. Still, a low-paying employer can survive. As a consequence of market friction, every employer has the power to set his or her own wage even when many competitors populate the market, and each will set a different wage to the extent that their circumstances differ.

The precise nature of the labor market equilibrium was not fully spelled out by either Mortensen or Phelps. As Rothschild (1973) asks, what is it that induces the wage dispersion that is supposed to motivate job search? Subsequently, papers by Butters (1977) and Burdett and Judd (1983) originally, followed by Mortensen (1990) and Burdett and Mortensen (1998) more recently, resolve the problem by formulating the model as a noncooperative price setting game played in a market characterized by search friction. In addition, these authors identify reasonable conditions such that dispersion in wage policy is the only equilibrium outcome of imperfect wage competition even when all workers and employers are identical. The essential logic of the argument follows.

Imagine that jobs are identical and that workers have a common reservation wage, employers offer wages, and each worker accepts at most one wage offer and rejects all the others. Friction exists in the market in the sense that workers do not know the wages offered by all employers. At any point in time, a worker possesses information about only a subset of the wages offered. Since all jobs are identical, a rational worker accepts the highest wage offer in the sample provided that it is above the common reservation wage. The typical employer, knowing these facts, realizes that her labor supply is not perfectly elastic even if she is only one among many employers for the following reasons. No offer below the reservation wage will be accepted. If the worker who receives the employer's wage offer has no other, then the worker will take any acceptable offer. If the worker who received her offer has another alternative, then the worker accepts only if the employer's offer is higher. More generally, any worker accepts a particular employer's offer only if it is the largest in that worker's sample of known offers.

Every employer's labor supply is upward sloping in her own wage offer for the reasons just given. However, there is no unique common equilibrium wage that all the identical employers will offer if the value of marginal product exceeds the workers' common reservation wage. If all employers offer the value of marginal product, a deviant can earn a positive expected profit at the margin by paying the lower reservation wage. If all employers offered the same wage and that wage is less than the worker's value of marginal product, then a deviant employer can guarantee that all the workers receiving her wage will accept it by offering only a penny more. Because the extra penny breaks all ties, an individual firm's supply correspondence jumps up discontinuously at the common wage offered by all of her competitors. Since deviating is more profitable in both cases, there is no symmetric pure strategy solution to this wage setting game.[5]

Butters (1977), Burdett and Judd (1983), and Mortensen (1990) all show that a unique mixed strategy equilibrium exists to different versions of the wage posting game. However, there are both theoretical and empirical objections to this interpretation of the wage dispersion observed. On the empirical side, the wage probability density implied by the theory is generally increasing and convex when in fact observed distributions are unimodal and skewed with a long right tail. On the theoretical side, one wonders how interfirm differences in wages offered across firms can persist if they simply reflect an incentive to randomize. How does the market find such an equilibrium?

Mortensen (1990), Burdett and Mortensen (1998), and Bontemps, Robin, and vanden Berg (1999) offer an answer to these questions. Specifically, they point out that more productive firms offer higher wages when the model is extended to allow for employer heterogeneity in worker productivity. In other words, if the same worker is more productive in one firm than in another, then the more productive firm finds it more profitable to compete by offering a higher wage. In the limiting case of a continuum of employer types, a unique pure strategy equilibrium exists for each firm. Furthermore, the distribution of wages offered converges to that corresponding to the case of homogenous employers as the diversity in labor productivity across employers vanishes. Because the distribution of wage offers across employers in part reflects the distribution of employer productivity, the extended model can match the shape of wage dispersion actually observed, at least in principle.

In closely related models of job and worker matching introduced by Diamond (1982), Mortensen (1982), and Pissarides (1985), worker and employer bargain over match rents attributable to market friction after they meet. This hypothesis is firmly embodied in the theory of equilibrium search unemployment as summarized in Pissarides (2000).[6] It too implies wage dispersion given productive heterogeneity across firms. Indeed, when embodied in a model of on-the-job search, its implications are very similar to those of the Burdett-Mortensen model.

The hypothesis that wage dispersion is largely the consequence of search friction and cross-firm differences in factor productivity is the organizing theme of the book. What are the implications of the hypothesis for worker and employer behavior? Are these implications consistent with data on worker flows and firm size? Is the distribution of employer productivity required to explain the wage dispersion observed plausible? Given productivity dispersion, are wages set by employing firms or are they bilateral bargaining outcomes? These are the kinds of questions that I try to answer.

The main body of the text is divided into several chapters. In chapter 1, more detailed evidence that similar workers are paid differently is provided, and a simple one-period model of wage dispersion designed to suggest explanations of the evidence is introduced. An intertemporal extension of the basic model, one that embodies the role of worker search behavior in the wage determination process, is the topic of chapter 2. Modifications of the theory that offer an explanation for the nature of observed wage dispersion, particularly the shape of the cross-firm distribution of average wages paid, are studied in chapter 3. In chapter 4, the hypothesis that firm wage policies are determined by profit-maximizing behavior is tested using Danish data and found wanting. Instead, bilateral bargaining outcomes are supported. Finally, recent work that extends the basic framework for the purpose of explaining intra-firm wage dispersion, particularly that associated with job tenure differences across workers, is reviewed in chapter 5.

Notes

1. See Katz and Autor (1999) and Katz and Murphy (1992) for detailed documentation of these facts.

2. See Abowd and Kramarz (1999) for descriptions of the matched employer-employee data sets currently available.

3. Manning (2001) provides a new and detailed exploration of the alternative implications of this kind of deviation from perfect competition.

4. Many thanks to George Neumann for reminding me of this passage. The fact that I had read it over forty years ago was clearly indicated by the underlining and the margin notes that I found in the text of my personal copy.

5. As Burdett and Judd (1983) show, the validity of this argument requires that some workers only receive one offer.

6. For reviews of recent developments and applications of both branches of the search equilibrium literature, see Mortensen and Pissarides (1999a,b).

1

Evidence in Search of Theory

If the law of one price were to hold in the labor market, similar workers would not be paid differently. In this chapter, I briefly review the evidence for wage dispersion. There are two kinds of empirical arguments. First, the fact that worker earnings are statistically associated with employer characteristics, particularly the employer's industry and size, is documented. Second, the results of recent attempts to measure worker and employer fixed effects in wage equations are reviewed.

In the second half of the chapter, a simple theory of wage dispersion is presented. The model used is a static one-period structure inspired by the work of Butters (1977) and Burdett and Judd (1983). The essential feature of the model is that workers have only partial information about employment opportunities. Given this fact, employers have monopsony power in the sense that a higher wage relative to those offered by competing employers will attract more workers. Because the extent to which a higher wage attracts workers depends only on its rank in the distribution of all offers, every individual employer has an incentive to differentiate its wage policy from those of all the others. Hence, wage dispersion is the outcome of the wage setting game that employers play with one another.

Although this structure alone generates wage dispersion, some form of employer heterogeneity is needed to explain convincingly the industry and size effects reported in the empirical literature on wage determination. The proposition that a worker's productivity depends on the employer's identity is natural in the context of the model for three interrelated reasons. First, more productive firms will both pay more and employ more workers. Second, employer heterogeneity cannot survive in a competitive labor market in the long run without search and recruiting friction. Third, cross-firm differences in factor productivity are commonplace in this environment.

The chapter concludes by considering other explanations of wage dispersion and their relationship to that studied here. These include compensating differentials, efficiency wages, and assortative matching. Although any and all of these may well provide complementary explanations, I argue that the theoretical plausibility of each as an explanation of wage dispersion is not greater than the simple hypothesis that wage policies vary with firm productivity.

1.1   The Evidence for Wage Dispersion

1.1.1   Size and Industry Differentials

The considerable variability in the average wage across industries and across firm size categories in the United States is reflected in table 1.1. Within size classes, average hourly earnings vary up to a factor of 2 across industries for each sex. The apparent premium associated with working for a large firm rather than a small one varies across industries

Table 1.1
Average hourly earnings (in USD) by industry, sex, and firm size (May 1983 CPS)

		In firms with an employment of		
Industry and sex	No. of workers	1–24	1000+	Ratio
Male				
Agriculture	4,667	4.388	6.436	1.467
Mining	12,369	8.316	13.487	1.622
Construction	9,380	7.995	13.679	1.711
Manufacturing	10,300	7.344	11.705	1.594
Trans./comm.	11,541	7.761	13.096	1.687
Trade	7,433	6.253	8.438	1.349
Finance	11,696	8.437	12.588	1.492
Services	8,677	7.526	10.020	1.331
Women				
Agriculture	4,696	4.556	5.013	1.100
Mining	9,606	9.917	9.706	0.979
Construction	6,687	6.344	8.262	1.302
Manufacturing	6,880	6.032	7.714	1.279
Trans./comm.	8,697	5.722	9.787	1.710
Trade	4,858	4.403	5.269	1.197
Finance	6,902	6.193	7.538	1.217
Services	6,656	5.955	7.759	1.303

Source: Oi and Idson (1999), Table 6.

from a low of 30 percent to high of about 70 percent for men. Similar differences exist for women. Although compensating differentials play some role in explaining cross-industry differences, "better jobs" seem to be concentrated in mining, finance, construction, and transportation/communication for both men and women, particularly in the larger firms of these industries.

Accounting for observable worker characteristics doesn't change the basic conclusions, as the results in table 1.2 illustrate. In the table, the log wage equation coefficients for industry and size variables obtained by Oi and Idson (1999) using the same May 1983 CPS data are reported. The wage equation is a standard one with size and industry dummies added

Table 1.2
Wage equation coefficients by sex, May 1983 CPS[a]

Variable	Male employees			Female employees		
	Mean	β	t-value	Mean	β	t-value
Firm/plant						
Size dummies[b]						
F2SP	0.030	0.110	3.96	0.032	0.088	3.06
F3SP	0.025	0.092	3.04	0.27	0.127	4.06
F4SP	0.008	0.147	2.76	0.007	0.048	0.83
F5SP	0.051	0.117	5.17	0.040	0.131	4.96
F2LP	0.115	0.087	5.32	0.116	0.075	4.41
F3LP	0.109	0.142	8.38	0.124	0.127	7.50
F4LP	0.043	0.134	5.53	0.055	0.160	7.00
F5LP	0.353	0.245	17.90	0.316	0.232	17.00
Industry						
Agriculture	0.025	−0.351	−11.28	0.005	−0.170	−2.40
Mining	0.024	0.193	6.31	0.005	0.326	4.69
Construction	0.084	0.186	9.91	0.012	0.079	1.70
Trans./comm.	0.094	0.103	6.08	0.055	0.161	6.86
Trade	0.216	−0.129	−9.53	0.240	−0.190	−12.44
Finance	0.055	0.031	1.43	0.119	−0.006	−0.35
Service	0.162	−0.112	−7.49	0.350	−0.026	−1.84
Statistics						
R^2	0.4064			0.3352		
N	7,833			5,973		

Source: Oi and Idson (1999), Table 9.
[a]Dependent variable is ln (hourly earnings).
[b]F2–F5 correspond to firm size categories 25–99, 100–499, 500–999, 1000+; SP, LP correspond to small plants (1–24) and large plants (25+), respectively.

as explanatory variables. Although the coefficient estimates are not reported here for the individual worker characteristics observed (for these, see Oi and Idson 1999), those included are the usual so-called human capital variables: education, linear and quadratic terms in experience and job tenure, and dummies for marital status, race, and location.

Although table 1.1 and table 1.2 tell a similar story about the importance of inter-industry and size differentials, several amendments can be noted once observable worker characteristics are taken into account. First, both industry and size differentials conditional on worker characteristics are somewhat smaller. This fact is consistent with the hypothesis that high-ability workers are generally employed in higher paying jobs. Second, the differences in the differentials across the two sexes suggested by the results reported in table 1.1 seem to disappear once human capital variables are included in the analysis.

Still, the results for both sexes imply large wage differences associated with the size and industry of the worker's employer. Indeed, the average worker in construction, mining, and transportation/communication industries earns from 16 to 33 percent more than the average manufacturing worker, while those in trade, services, and agriculture earn 10 to 35 percent less. Moreover, the 30 to 35 percent of the work force employed in the largest firm/plant size category earn 24 percent more than the 20 percent or so who work in single plant firms with fewer than twenty-five employees. By way of comparison, four years of higher education are associated with 25 percent additional earning given the authors' estimate of the years of education coefficient. Finally, note that the variance explained as measured by the R^2 statistic is barely over 40 percent for men and only about 35 percent for women even when size and industry are included. Hence, there is still considerable wage dispersion left to be explained.

1.1.2 Decomposing Size and Industry Differentials

Following Abowd, Kramarz, and Margolis (1999) and Abowd and Kramarz (2000a,b), consider a linear statistical wage equation model of the form

$$y_{it} = \alpha_i + \gamma_{J(i,t)} + x_{it}\beta + \varepsilon_{it}, \tag{1.1}$$

where y_{it} is a measure of the difference between worker i's compensation in period t and the overall mean, x_{it} is the vector representing time varying worker characteristics as the differences between worker i's observable characteristics in period t and the overall mean vector of worker characteristics, and ε_{it} is the residual assumed to be orthogonal to all the other effects in the model and zero on average. The interpretations of the parameters of the model follow: α_i is a fixed worker effect, γ_j is a fixed employer effect where $j = J(i, t)$ is the employer of worker i in period t, and β is a vector of worker characteristic coefficients.

As Abowd and his coauthors point out, a true industry (or size) effect is an average of the firm effect parameters over the firm's in the industry (size class) of interest given the model described by equation (1.1). However, most studies cannot identify the fixed effects because employer identities are not available in the data sets used to estimate the model. Instead, observable employer characteristics, industry, and size typically are included as in the Oi and Idson study discussed in the previous section. In the case of industry effects, the model estimated is of the form

$$y_{it} = \kappa^*_{K(J(i,t))} + x_{it}\beta^* + u_{it},$$

where the function $k = K(j)$ represents the industry of firm j (or size class) and κ_k is what Abowd and his coauthors refer to as the "raw" wage effect of industry (size class) k. Clearly, the estimate of the industry (size) effect obtained is equal to an appropriately weighted average of the industry's worker and firm fixed effects.

The matrix form of the stacked system of equation defined in (1.1) is

$$y = D\alpha + F\gamma + X\beta + \varepsilon, \tag{1.2}$$

where D is design matrix for the worker effect and F is the design matrix for the employer effect. Specifically, each column of D is a vector associated with a particular worker, say i, with row element equal to one if the worker i is the observed worker and zero otherwise, and each column of F is analogously defined for each employer j. According to Abowd and his coauthors, the raw inter-industry effect vector is

$$\kappa^* = (A'F'M_XF A)^{-1} A'F M_X D\alpha + (A'F'M_XF A)^{-1} A'F M_X F\gamma \tag{1.3}$$

if equation (1.2) represents the true model, where A is the matrix that maps firms into industries and

$$M_X = I - X(X'X)^{-1}X'.$$

The two terms of (1.3) represent the decomposition of the raw industry effect into the sum of the industry-average worker effect and industry-average employer effect conditional on X. Since the worker effect can be interpreted as returns to ability, it is the employer effect that reflects wage dispersion as I have defined it.

Using matched employer-employee quarterly data for France and the state of Washington, Abowd and Kramarz (2000a,b) first estimate the individual worker and firm effects and then use these estimates to compute industry-average worker and employer effects conditional on observable worker characteristics for two-digit SIC industry classifications. Next, they verify that equation (1.3) holds for their data in the statistical sense that a regression of the worker and employer industry-average effects on the raw industry differentials across industries generates regression coefficients estimates equal to unity for both effects and an R^2 in excess of 0.98. Finally, as a measure of the relative importance of each of the two industry-average effects as an explanation of the industry differentials, they compute and report the weighted proportion of the raw industry effect explained by each component on the right side of (1.3). According to this measure, the two effects are equally important. Specifically in Abowd, Creecy, and Kramarz (2002), the authors conclude that 45 percent of the industry differential in the French data and 50 percent in the Washington state data is wage dispersion as I have defined it earlier while the other half can be attributed to unobserved worker ability differences across industries.

By reinterpreting $k = 1, 2, \ldots$ as size categories rather than industries, the same methodology applies to firm size differentials. Namely, the raw size differentials too can be decomposed into industry-average worker and employer effects as represented by equation (1.3). In this case, 71 percent of the raw size differential in the Washington state data and 76 percent in the French data are explained by cross-firm wage dispersion after both observed and unobserved worker ability are accounted for.

These studies imply that wage dispersion is a consequence of both unobserved worker and employer characteristics. Interestingly, Abowd and his coauthors provide evidence that the two unobserved components are not correlated as sorting arguments might suggest. Specifically, Abowd, Kramarz, and Margolis (1999) estimate a correlation between firm and worker effects of 0.08 in the French DADS panel, and Abowd, Finer, and Kramarz (1999) find that the correlation coefficient is essentially zero in the Washington data. In their most recent report based on exact computation methods rather than the approximation methods used in their earlier work, Abowd, Creecy, and Kramarz (2002) find that the correlation between the estimated worker and firm fixed effects are slightly negative for both data sets.

1.1.3   Size Differences in Average Wages Paid

Information on average wages that firms pay in the United States is still relatively scarce. However, Davis and Haltiwanger (1991, 1996), using evidence that matches CPS data on the earnings of individual workers with the identity of the manufacturing establishment employing them found in the LRD, have documented a number of interesting and relevant facts about the level and growth in wage-size effects and wage dispersion across plants. Consistent with other studies, they find that the production worker average real wage differential between plants employing more than 5,000 employees and plants with twenty to forty-nine employees was $3.40 per hour (1982 dollars) in 1967 while the average hourly wage paid overall was $8.18. However, during the 1967 and 1986 period, which saw the hourly average rise by only one (1982) dollar, the differential grew to $6.31 per hour. This increase accounted for 40 percent of the increase in between-plant wage dispersion, and the between-plant component in turn accounts for 48 percent in the overall growth in manufacturing wage variance. In 1982, the variance in mean wages across plants accounted for 59 percent of total variance while the within-plant variance accounts for only 2 percent. Finally, although the mean wage paid increases at an increasing rate with plant size, wage dispersion falls sharply with size.

1.2   Search Theories of Wage Dispersion

Having made the case for the existence of differences in wages paid across employers, I turn to a consideration of possible explanations. Equilibrium search and efficiency wage theories provide useful tools for the analysis of price determination in the presence of frictions. Given the importance of friction in labor markets, it is no surprise that much of the literature in this area is on wage dispersion.

There are at least three different branches of the search theoretic approach to wage dispersion. Albrecht and Axel (1984) suppose that workers have different reservations wages. Given this form of supply-side heterogeneity, some employers choose a high wage policy and hire all worker types while others pay low wages with the expectation that they will hire only workers with low reservation wages. If employers are identical, both strategies earn the same profit in equilibrium. Wage dispersion is a strategic outcome of wage competition in Butters (1977) and Burdett and Judd (1983). Although there is no need for differences in reservation wages in their framework, one can easily extend the models to incorporate them. Arguably the best-known branch of equilibrium search theory is represented by the bilateral bargaining or rent sharing approach to wage determination in search markets pioneered by Diamond (1982), Mortensen (1982), and Pissarides (1985). As I demonstrate, this hypothesis has very similar qualitative implications.

Consider an economy composed of fixed numbers of identical employers and identical job-seeking workers. Time consists of a single period and all workers are unemployed initially. Employers possess a linear technology relating the number of workers employed to output. Both workers and employers are expected income maximizers. Friction exists in the sense that no worker knows the wage paid by any employer at the beginning of the period. Although each employing firm has an incentive to inform workers of its wage, its capacity to do so is limited. Specifically, each firm randomly mails a number of offers, a small number relative to the number of workers in the market, to a subset of workers. Once imperfectly informed in this way, each worker applies for the highest-paying job among the offers received. Finally, each employer, realizing that workers can receive more than one offer, sets a wage taking into account the similar incentives of the other competing employers to hire the worker. As previously noted, the only equilibrium solution to this game generates a distribution of offers even when employers are all identical.

1.2.1 Pure Wage Dispersion

I begin with a demonstration of the claim that the equilibrium solution to the wage posting game sketched earlier implies wage dispersion even when all workers and firms are identical. There are m employers and n workers in the economy. The output of a job-worker match is independent of both the worker's and employer's identity. Assume constant returns to scale in production in the sense that the common marginal revenue product of labor is a constant denoted as p. Every worker prefers employment at a higher wage but is willing to work for any wage no less than the common reservation wage, denoted as b. An employer makes a profit by employing a worker if and only if the wage paid, w, is no greater than p. Hence, in the only interesting case, $p > b$.

If wage information can be communicated costlessly, Bertrand competition among employers yields a market wage equal to marginal labor productivity, p, in this simple world. To capture the idea that communication between a large number of workers and any employer is incomplete, assume initially that an employer can contact just one worker and the message sent informs the worker of employment terms. Since the employer knows all workers are identical, the particular worker chosen as the recipient is picked at random. Obviously, if a worker receives only one offer, it will be accepted if and only if its value w is no less than the worker's reservation wage. However, if two or more acceptable offers are received, then the worker chooses the job that pays the highest wage. Suppose that in the case of a tie, the worker selects the job to accept at random among those offering the highest wage.

The employer knows that the worker will accept the highest-paying offer as described previously but can not know the number of or the values of the other offers that the particular worker contacted will receive. Hence, she can only compute the probability of acceptance given the offers of all employers as summarized by the offer distribution. Since every employer's payoff depends on the distributions of wages offered by all other employers, the wage determination problem is a noncooperative game.

Formally, the game has two stages. First, all employers simultaneously choose a wage offer and then communicate it to a worker drawn at random. In the second stage, each worker accepts the best offer from among those received. To formulate the payoff of any employer in the market, one needs to know only the probability that the worker contacted will accept any prospective offer. This fact implies that the game is rather special. Namely, there is no symmetric pure strategy solution, because only an offer's rank order matters.

Since any worker can be contacted by each firm, the total number of offers actually received by a particular worker, call it X, is binomially distributed with "probability of success" equal to the probability of a contact by a particular message, $1/n$, and "sample size" equal to the total number of messages sent by all employers, which is equal to the number of employers, m, in this example. It is convenient to use the fact that the binomial is approximated by the Poisson with mean $\lambda = m/n$ when both n and m are large. In other words, in large markets, the distribution over the number of offers received is

$$\Pr\{X = x\} = \frac{e^{-\lambda}\lambda^x}{x!}, \quad \text{where } \lambda = \frac{m}{n} \tag{1.4}$$

is the expected number of contacts made per worker in the market, hereafter called the contact frequency.[1]

In what follows I show that the probability that a worker accepts a wage offer w depends only on the contact frequency, λ, and the offer's rank as represented by the fraction of other offers that are no greater than w, the c.d.f. $F(w)$. Denote the probability of acceptance as $P(F(w), \lambda)$. The expected profit attributable to contacting a worker given a wage offer equal to w and wage offer distribution function $F(w)$ is simply the product of the acceptance probability and the difference between the value of output and the wage paid, that is,

$$\pi(p, w, F(w)) = P(F(w), \lambda)(p - w). \tag{1.5}$$

As a first step in the analysis of the game, let me formally establish that there is no symmetric pure strategy equilibrium. For, if all other employers were to offer the same wage and that wage w is strictly less than the worker's value to a firm p, then a deviant can earn more profit with certainty for any small positive deviation $\varepsilon > 0$ because the worker contacted will accept the offer for sure. Because the probability of employing the worker contacted, denoted as q, is strictly less than unity were the employer to conform by paying w, it always pays to deviate, that is, $p - (w + \varepsilon) > q(p - w) > 0$ for all ε sufficiently small because $q < 1$. To prove formally that the probability that the worker contacted will be hired is less than unity when all offer the same wage, simply note that probability that x other firms will also contact the same worker is given by (1.4). Since the worker selects an employer at random from the set when all offer the same wage,

$$q = \sum_{x=0}^{\infty} \left(\frac{1}{1+x} \right) \frac{e^{-\lambda} \lambda^x}{x!} = \frac{1}{\lambda} \sum_{x=0}^{\infty} \frac{e^{-\lambda} \lambda^{x+1}}{(x+1)!}$$

$$= \frac{1}{\lambda} \sum_{x=1}^{\infty} \frac{e^{-\lambda} \lambda^x}{x!} = \frac{1 - e^{-\lambda}}{\lambda} < 1$$

for all $0 < \lambda < \infty$. An analogous argument rules out any equilibrium in pure strategies in which some strictly positive fraction of the employers offer the same wage.

Of course, if all employers were to offer $w = p$, then none would deviate by offering a higher wage because doing so would generate a negative profit with certainty. But, in this case, a deviant can earn an expected positive profit by simply offering the reservation wage b because the probability that the worker contacted will receive no other offer, equal to $e^{-\lambda}$, is strictly positive.

Since only those workers who receive one offer accept the lowest wage in the market and because the set of employers who make the offer is not a mass point by the previous argument, the lower support of the distribution is the reservation wage b. Formally, the probability of hiring the worker contacted is $e^{-\lambda}$ if $\underline{w} \geq b$, which implies

$$\underline{w} = \arg\max_{w \geq b} \pi(p, w, 0) = \arg\max_{w \geq b} e^{-\lambda}(p - w) = b. \tag{1.6}$$

Because all equilibrium offers must generate the same profit, there is no gap in the support of an equilibrium offer distribution. If there were, say between (w', w'') where $w'' > w'$ and w'' is in the support of an optimal wage strategy, then one obtains the contradiction

$$\pi(p, w, F(w)) > \pi(p, w'', F(w'')) \quad \text{for all } w \in (w', w'')$$

because $F(w'') = F(w')$. Finally, the upper support is no greater than p since any employer can guarantee no expected loss by choosing $w = p$.

Proposition 1. Any equilibrium market distribution of offers, represented by the c.d.f. $F(w)$, is continuous, has a connected support, is bounded below by b, and has upper support less than p.[2]

Given any candidate for an equilibrium, a continuous c.d.f. $F : [b, p] \rightarrow [0, 1]$, the acceptance probability function $P(F(w), \lambda)$ can be derived as follows. The probability that an offer w exceeds the x other offers received by the worker contacted is the probability that all alternatives are less than w, equal to $F(w)^x$. Hence, the number of other offers received, x, is a Poisson variable characterized in (1.4),

$$P(F(w), \lambda) = \sum_{x=0}^{\infty} F(w)^x \frac{e^{-\lambda}\lambda^x}{x!}$$

$$= e^{-\lambda[1-F(w)]} \sum_{x=0}^{\infty} \frac{e^{-\lambda F(w)}(\lambda F(w))^x}{x!} = e^{-\lambda[1-F(w)]} \tag{1.7}$$

for any equilibrium candidate. The acceptance probably is continuous and increasing in w, because a higher relative wage increases the chance that it will be the highest offer received by the worker contacted, and is continuous and decreasing in the offer arrival frequency, because the number of alternative offers stochastically increases with λ.

In choosing a wage offer, an employer trades off a lower expected profit given an acceptance against a higher probability of acceptance.

Since all offers are profit maximizing, these two effects of a higher wage must be equal everywhere on the support of an equilibrium wage offer distribution. In other words, the equilibrium offer distribution must satisfy

$$\pi(p, w, F(w)) = (p - w)e^{-\lambda[1-F(w)]} =$$
$$\pi(p, b, 0) = (p - b)e^{-\lambda} \quad \text{for all } w \in [b, \overline{w}].$$

Equivalently, the closed form solution for the unique equilibrium offer c.d.f. is

$$F(w) = \frac{1}{\lambda} \log\left(\frac{p-b}{p-w}\right), \tag{1.8}$$

where the upper support is

$$\overline{w} = (1 - e^{-\lambda})p + e^{-\lambda}b. \tag{1.9}$$

Because these results imply that $F(w) \to 0$ for any $w < p$ and $\overline{w} \to p$ as $\lambda \to \infty$, the solution to the classic Bertrand competition model is the limit of the search equilibrium derived here as the contact frequency per worker tends to infinity. In other words, if there were no limit on the number of workers each employer could contact, all wage offers equal marginal product as implied by perfect competition. Most of the models studied in the rest of this book have this property.

Although the model offers an explanation for wage dispersion, which firm adopts which wage policy is arbitrary. In particular, wage effects associated with size class and industry affiliation are not explained by the model in its simplest form. However, wage differentials of both kinds are consistent with the model when labor productivity differs across employers. In this generalization, different wage policies are associated with employers of different types.

1.2.2   Inter-Industry Differentials
As Oi and Idson (1999) point out, labor productivity varies across industries and, indeed, across firms within industries. Certainly, any indicator of labor productivity—say, value added per worker—differs considerably across firms. Just why these differences exist and seem to persist is a subject of considerable discussion. Some argue that productive heterogeneity reflects differences in employer power in their output markets. Others emphasize differences in fixed factors of production. For

example, both management skills and corporate cultures differ across firms, and these differences may cluster by industry. The dynamic processes of creative destruction and of learning about productivity can also induce differences across employers. Whatever the reason, the following argument demonstrates that our simple wage determination model implies a positive cross-firm correlation between the wage paid and the productivity of labor.

Suppose participating employers are different with respect to the productivity of their work force. I need to show that the profit maximizing wage offered by any employer of the higher productivity type is no less than that offered by a lower productivity type. Conditional on the employer's labor productivity p, the wage offered by the employer w, and the distribution of wages offered in the market $F(w)$, expected profit per worker contacted is

$$\pi(p, w, F(w)) = P(F(w), \lambda)(p - w), \tag{1.10}$$

where $P(F(w), \lambda)$ is the probability that the worker contacted will accept a wage offer equal to w, defined in equation (1.7). The set of optimal wage choice is

$$w(p) = \arg\max_{w \geq b} \pi(p, w, F(w)), \tag{1.11}$$

and

$$\pi^*(p) = \max_{w \geq b} \pi(p, w, F(w)) = \max_{w \geq b} e^{-\lambda[1-F(w)]}(p - w) \tag{1.12}$$

represents the associated maximal expected profit per worker contacted for a type p firm.

Proposition 2. Given any two firms, the more productive offers a higher wage and expects a strictly greater profit per worker contacted, that is, $p'' > p' \Rightarrow \pi^*(p'') > \pi^*(p')$ and $w'' \geq w'$ for any $w'' \in w(p'')$ and $w' \in w(p')$.

Proof. Given $p'' > p'$, $w'' \in w(p'')$, and $w' \in w(p')$

$$\pi^*(p'') = P(F(w''), \lambda)(p'' - w'')$$

$$\geq P(F(w'), \lambda)(p'' - w')$$

$$> P(F(w'), \lambda)(p' - w') = \pi^*(p')$$

$$\geq P(F(w''), \lambda)(p' - w''). \tag{1.13}$$

The two equalities follow from the definitions (1.11) and (1.12), the weak inequalities are implied by the assumption that the wages w'' and w' are profit maximizing choices for any employer of type p'' and p', respectively, and the strict inequality is implied by $p'' > p'$. One obvious consequence of these inequalities is that the more productive firm makes strictly more profit on average. The other,

$$(p'' - p')P(F(w''), \lambda) \geq (p'' - p')P(F(w'), \lambda) > 0, \tag{1.14}$$

implies that $w'' \geq w'$ because $P(F(w), \lambda)$ is strictly increasing in w from equation (1.7).

In other words, any element of the set of optimal wage choices for the more productive type is no smaller than any element of the set of optimal wage choices for the less productive type. It follows that the intersection of the supports of the equilibrium offers made by two types of firms with adjacent productivity levels contains at most the single wage representing the boundary between them. Indeed, because the probability of acceptance depends only on the rank order of the wage offered, not on its magnitude, the lower bound on the set of wages offered by the more productive must be the upper bound on the set offered by the next most productive type for the same reason that there can be no gap in the support for a given type. Namely, if there were a gap, the more productive employer offering the lowest wage for her type could make a larger profit by offering a slightly lower wage.[3]

For example, in the case of two firm types represented by p_1 and p_2 where $p_2 > p_1$, the lowest wage offered by a type 1 employer is the workers' common reservation wage, $\underline{w}_1 = b$, and the lowest wage offered by a type 2 employer is the highest wage paid by a type 1 employer, $\overline{w}_1 = \underline{w}_2$. Because profit must be equal across employers of the same type in the sense that $\pi^*(p_1) = P(F(b), \lambda)(p_1 - b) = P(F(w), \lambda)(p_1 - w)$ for all $w \in [b, \overline{w}_1]$ and $\pi^*(p_2) = P(F(\overline{w}_1), \lambda)(p_2 - \underline{w}_2) = P(F(w), \lambda)(p_2 - w)$ for all $w \in [\underline{w}_2, \overline{w}_2]$ where $\overline{w}_2$ is the largest offer of a type 2 employer, equations (1.6), (1.7), and (1.10) imply that the equilibrium distribution takes the form

$$F(w) = \begin{cases} \frac{1}{\lambda} \ln\left(\frac{p_1 - b}{p_1 - w}\right) & \text{for } w \in w(p_1) = [b, \overline{w}_1] \\ \frac{1}{\lambda} \ln\left(\frac{p_2 - \underline{w}_2}{p_2 - w}\right) & \text{for } w \in w(p_2) = [\underline{w}_2, \overline{w}_2] \end{cases} \tag{1.15}$$

where $\overline{w}_1 = \underline{w}_2$ in the case of two types. The upper supports of the sets of offers made by the two employer types are the unique solutions to

$$F(\overline{w}_1) = \frac{1}{\lambda} \ln \left(\frac{p_1 - b}{p_1 - \overline{w}_1} \right) = q$$

$$F(\overline{w}_2) = \frac{1}{\lambda} \ln \left(\frac{p_2 - \overline{w}_1}{p_2 - \overline{w}_2} \right) = 1$$

(1.16)

given that here q represents the fraction of the employers who are of type 1. One can easily generalize this characterization of the equilibrium to any countable number of types.

In equilibrium, then, wage offers are positively correlated with labor productivity across employers in this extension of the model. Hence, they provide an explanation for an employer fixed effect in any wage equation. Furthermore, if average productivity differences exist across industries, then identical workers in industries with higher labor productivity earn more.

1.2.3   Firm-Size Differentials

In the examples so far, each employer contacts only a single worker by assumption. But in the equilibrium characterized earlier, a high-productivity employer has an incentive to attract more workers than does a low-productivity employer because the expected profit made on the marginal worker contacted is larger. Consequently, a generalization of the basic model that endogenizes recruiting effort will generate a positive correlation among the wage paid, recruiting effort, and firm size.

Let v represent the number of workers contacted, a measure of recruiting effort, and let $c(v)$ represent an increasing and convex cost of recruiting. Given the distribution of wage offers in the market and the employer's wage offer, a type p employer's expected gross profit is then given by

$$\pi(p, w, F(w))v - c(v),$$

the difference between the gross expected profit from recruiting activity and its cost. Because different firms of the same type will generally offer different wage rates for reasons that are now understood, the first-order condition suggests that the optimal choice of recruiting effort depends on both firm productivity type and particular wage paid. However, this conjecture is false. To prove the assertion, simply note that the total expected profit of a type p employer given an optimal choice of both the wage and recruiting effort is

$$\max_{w \geq b, v \geq 0} \{\pi(p, w, F(w))v - c(v)\}$$

$$= \max_{v \geq 0} \left\{ \max_{w \geq b} \{\pi(p, w, F(w))\}v - c(v) \right\}$$

$$= \max_{v \geq 0} \{\pi^*(p)v - c(v)\},$$

where $\pi^*(p)$ is the common maximal expected profit per worker contacted by any employer of productivity type p defined in (1.12). Hence, the unique optimal number of contacts made by all employers of type p, denoted $v(p)$, solves

$$c'(v(p)) = \pi^*(p) \tag{1.17}$$

given the following additional regularity conditions: $c(0) = c'(0) = 0$ and $\lim_{v \to \infty} c'(v) = \infty$.

As previously established, the expected profit per worker contacted is strictly larger for a more productive firm. Hence, a more productive employer contacts more workers, that is, $p'' > p'$ implies $v(p'') > v(p')$ by (1.17) and (1.13) given the second-order condition $c''(v) > 0$. Because an employer's firm size equals the number of acceptances out of the v workers contacted, the expected size of a more productive employer, equal to $n(p) = P(F(w(p)), \lambda)v(p)$, is larger both because the number of workers contacted is larger and because the probability of acceptance is higher. Finally, as firms of the same type choose different wage offers but all are higher than the wages offered by a less productive type, the wage paid is positively but not perfectly correlated with realized firm size.

The observant reader will have realized that equilibrium is more complex in this extension of the basic model because the total number of workers contacted by all firms is endogenous. Although the equilibrium wage offer distribution satisfied equation (1.15), the first equation of (1.16) must be replaced by

$$F(\overline{w}_1) = \frac{1}{\lambda} \ln \left(\frac{p_1 - b}{p_1 - \overline{w}_1} \right) = \frac{q v(p_1)}{q v(p_1) + (1 - q)v(p_2)} \tag{1.18}$$

and

$$F(\overline{w}_2) = \frac{1}{\lambda} \ln \left(\frac{p_2 - \overline{w}_1}{p_2 - \overline{w}_2} \right) = 1, \tag{1.19}$$

where q is the fraction of type p_1 employers in the case of two types because each employer of type p_i contacts $v_i = v(p_i)$ workers and $F(\overline{w}_1)$ equals the fraction of contacts made by type 1 firms. In addition, the aggregate contact frequency is given by

$$\lambda = \frac{m}{n}[qv(p_1) + (1-q)v(p_2)], \tag{1.20}$$

where m and n are the total numbers of employers and workers respectively. Finally, the first-order condition for an optimal choice of recruiting effort and the equal profit per worker contacted condition for each employer type imply

$$c'(v(p_1)) = \pi^*(p_1) = e^{-\lambda}(p_1 - b) \tag{1.21}$$

and

$$c'(v(p_2)) = \pi^*(p_2) = p_2 - \overline{w}_2. \tag{1.22}$$

The equilibrium wage offer distribution given λ, $\overline{w}_1$, $\overline{w}_2$, $v(p_1)$ and $v(p_2)$ solves equations (1.18)–(1.22). With a little algebra, one can show that a unique nonnegative equilibrium solution exists provided that $p_2 > p_1 \geq b$.

Note that a rising marginal cost of recruiting is essential for the existence of differences in employer productivity in equilibrium. If the cost were instead linear, only employers of the most productive type actually participate by contacting workers. This result follows by virtue of the fact that the contact frequency of the most productive type will be finite only if the constant marginal cost, $c = c'(v)$, is equal to the expected profit per worker for the most productive type. But, if this condition holds, then $c = \pi^*(p_2) > \pi^*(p_1)$, which implies that the less productive type cannot afford to recruit workers.

1.2.4 Bilateral Bargaining

The hypothesis that the wage paid is set by the employer is but one element in a class of wage determination models that fall under the general heading of "rent sharing" where the shared rents are those induced by market friction. The assumption that worker and employer bargain over these rents after they meet is an obvious alternative to the monopsony hypothesis. Indeed, such is the prevailing specification in most of the search equilibrium literature. (See Pissarides (2000) and Mortensen and Pissarides (1999a,b).) One can easily verify that differences in labor productivity can explain both industry and size effects under this hypothesis as well.

The rent to be shared by any pair once they meet is the difference between the productivity of a match p and the alternative income that the worker could earn were he not employed, b. Since b represents the worker's "outside option," the generalized Nash equilibrium solution for firm with productivity p is

$$w(p) = \arg\max_w (p - w)^{1-\beta}(w - b)^{\beta} = b + \beta(p - b), \qquad (1.23)$$

where $\beta \in (0, 1)$ represents the worker's "bargaining power." Since $p'' > p'$ implies $w(p'') \geq w(p')$ in this case as well, industries composed of more productive firms offer a positive wage premium.

A positive size differential is implied by the following first-order condition for optimal recruiting effort:

$$c'(v(p)) = \pi(w(p), F(w(p))) = P(F(w(p)), \lambda)(p - w(p))$$

$$= e^{-\lambda[1-F(b+\beta(p-b))]}(1 - \beta)(p - b). \qquad (1.24)$$

In other words, more productive firms invest more in recruiting effort in the sense that $p'' > p'$ implies $v(p'') > v(p')$ given $c''(v) > 0$.

1.3 Other Theories of Wage Dispersion

1.3.1 Compensating Differentials

Compensating differentials are also a source of wage dispersion reflected in the firm fixed effect of the statistical model assumed by Abowd and his coauthors. For example, the large premium for mining apparent in table 1.2 suggests that differentials of this form contribute to their explanation. However, except for occupational risk of injury and death, compensating differentials are generally hard to find empirically. Futhermore, job amenities, both benefits and creature comforts on the job, are positively associated with wages received across jobs, not negatively correlated as the pure theory of compensating differential suggests. Hwang, Mortensen, and Reed (1998) and Lang and Mujumdar (1999) show that these facts can also be explained by an extension of the search model introduced earlier.

Let a represent a job characteristic that is desirable in the sense that each worker values it as well as the wage paid. Formally, let $u(w, a)$, an increasing function in both arguments, represent the utility of a job characterized by the wage-amenity pair (w, a). Given this structure, a worker accepts the offer received that yields the greatest utility. Next, assume that all workers have the same preference. Let $F(u)$ represent the fraction of jobs that offer utility u or less, and let $P(F(u), \lambda)$ represent the probability that a randomly contacted offer is accepted as defined by equation (1.7).

Assume that job amenities can be provided at a cost $c(a)$. The firm then chooses the wage-amenity pair to maximize expected profit. Since the cost is incurred only if the worker accepts the offered pair,

$$(w, a) = \arg \max_{(w,a) \geq (b, 0)} \{P(F(u(a, w)), \lambda)[p - w - c(a)]\}. \tag{1.25}$$

The first-order condition for an interior choice,

$$\frac{u_a(w, a)}{u_w(w, a)} = c'(a), \tag{1.26}$$

implies that the pair minimizes total compensation, the sum $w + c(a)$, given the overall utility of a job provided to a worker. Under the standard assumption that the utility function is quasi-concave in wage and amenity and the cost of supplying the amenity is convex, the tangency condition implies a monotone increasing relation between the wage and amenity given that both are "normal" goods in the standard sense. In other words, across employers offering jobs of different utility levels, the job paying more also provides more job amenity if workers prefer both more pay and more desirable working conditions as the utility of the pair increases. Let $(w(u), a(u))$ represent the locus of points defined by (1.26).

Again, no positive fraction of employers will offer the same utility because a deviant can do better by creating a slightly better job. Because all identical employers must earn the same profit, the distribution of utility across employers, as characterized by the c.d.f. $F(u)$, solves the equal profit condition

$$\pi(u, F(u), \lambda) = P(F(u), \lambda)[p - w(u) - c(a(u))]$$

$$= P(0, \lambda)[p - w(b) - c(a(b))] = \pi(b, 0, \lambda),$$

where now b represents the reservation utility required to induce a worker to accept employment. From equation (1.7), the equilibrium distribution of utility is

$$F(u) = \frac{1}{\lambda} \ln \left(\frac{p - w(b) - c(a(b))}{p - w(u) - c(a(u))} \right). \tag{1.27}$$

As total compensation $w(u) + c(a(u))$ increases with u whether or not a and u are both normal goods, the only equilibrium candidate is a legitimate c.d.f. Finally, the most desirable job offer represented by utility level $\bar{u}$ solves

$$F(\bar{u}) = 1 = \frac{1}{\lambda} \ln \left(\frac{p - w(b) - c(a(b))}{p - w(\bar{u}) - c(a(\bar{u}))} \right).$$

In sum, the equilibrium locus of wage and amenity combinations that identical employers would provide is upward sloping if earnings and amenities are normal goods, rather than downward sloping as the theory of compensating differential would imply. Of course, the latter theory does come into play when either employers differ with respect to labor productivity or the cost of supplying job amenities. In this case, the locus of wage-amenity pairs for each employer type is positively sloped for the reason described previously but the sets offered by different types would generally be negatively associated given the worker's willingness to trade more amenity for a lower wage. Which effect dominates empirically depends on the extent of employer heterogeneity. These facts weaken the argument that compensating differentials alone can explain the employer fixed effects apparent in matched employer-employee data.

1.3.2 Efficiency Wage
Another explanation of wage dispersion found in the literature arises out of the need to motivate worker effort. For example, in the Shapiro and Stiglitz (1984) shirking model, employers threaten to fire any worker found performing below some threshold but only monitor individual worker effort at random on occasion for cost reasons. To make the threat effective, a wage above the worker's immediate outside option must be paid. Following this logic, Bulow and Summers (1986) argue that inter-industry differences in the costs and benefits of monitoring worker effort can explain why the wages of observably similar workers vary across sectors of the economy. Presumably the same argument applies in the case of size differentials.

Although it may be plausible to imagine that larger firms find it more costly to monitor effort and, consequently, must pay a higher efficiency wage, I find it difficult to understand why this argument applies to observed industry differentials. Furthermore, experience as well as direct evidence suggests that interfirm variation in wages swamps cross-industry variation. Is one to believe that these differences are due to idiosyncratic cross-firm differences in monitoring technology?

One can easily incorporate the essence of the shirking model into the basic single-period search model. However, once one does so, the force of the argument as an explanation for wage dispersion is somewhat weakened because employed workers collect surplus anyway when search friction is present. Imagine that employers face different monitoring technologies and as a consequence some monitor more frequently than others. In particular, let $1 > \eta_1 > \eta_2$ where here η_i represents the monitoring probability for type i employers. All employers are equally productive, and the common marginal product is denoted as p as in the basic model. As before the alternative to employment is unemployment, which "pays" the value of leisure b. Now for simplicity suppose that a shirking worker, if not caught, collects both the value of leisure and the wage. Then, in order to have an incentive not to shirk, the wage offered by a type i employer must satisfy the incentive compatibility condition

$$w \geq \eta_i b + (1 - \eta_i)(b + w).$$

In other words, the wage earned given no shirking must exceed the expected income equivalent when shirking. Equivalently,

$$w \geq b/\eta_i > b. \tag{1.28}$$

The incentive constraint for the type with the higher monitoring frequency clearly determines the lower support of the equilibrium offer distribution in the sense that now $\underline{w} = b/\eta_1 > b$, rather than the reservation wage, is the lowest wage paid. Of course, equal profit still requires that

$$F(w) = \frac{1}{\lambda} \ln \left(\frac{p - b/\eta_1}{p - w} \right) \quad \text{for all } w \in [b/\eta_1, \overline{w}_1], \tag{1.29}$$

where

$$F(\overline{w}_1) = q \tag{1.30}$$

and q is the fraction of firms of type η_1.

For the low monitoring probability type, two cases exist: Either the incentive constraint determines the lowest wage offered by a member firm or the constraint is not binding. Since in the latter case, the profit earned is the same for both types, it follows that

$$F(w) = \frac{1}{\lambda} \ln \left(\frac{p - w_2}{p - w} \right) \quad \text{for all } w \in [\underline{w}_2, \overline{w}_2],$$ (1.31)

where

$$\underline{w}_2 = \max \left\langle \frac{b}{\eta_2}, \overline{w}_1 \right\rangle \quad \text{and} \quad F(\overline{w}_2) = 1.$$

In other words, if $\overline{w}_1 \geq b/\eta_2$, then those with a low monitoring probability do not have to pay an efficiency wage and are as profitable as the
other firms. They simply locate in the upper range of the equilibrium
support. By implication, there is a gap in the support of the equilibrium
offer distribution and, consequently, the type with the low monitoring
probability make less profit if and only if the incentive constraint is
binding, that is, $\overline{w}_1 < b/\eta_2$.

In sum, the monitoring problem will raise the lowest wage paid in
equilibrium but will not contribute to the differentials that already exist
across firms if differences in monitoring probabilities are small. This
conclusion follows from the fact that the incentive constraint does not
bind if the highest wage paid by the next higher monitoring probability
type is high enough. Whether or not the constraint binds depends both
on the distribution of firms by type and on the differences in monitoring
probabilities.

1.3.3   Sorting

Murphy and Topel (1990) argue that higher-paying firms employ more
able workers. As Becker (1973) points out, heterogenous workers and
employers are matched so as to maximize the value of total output in
a perfectly competitive equilibrium solution to the binary assignment
problem. If the available number of jobs are fixed and each requires
one worker to be productive, and if worker and employer abilities
are complementary in production, then the maximum value of output condition implies that more able workers are matched with more
productive employers in a perfectly competitive equilibrium. Shimer
and Smith (2000) show that worker and employer productivities are
positively associated in a random matching market where pairs meet
sequentially over time and share match rents although the conditions
for the form of positive assortative matching they study are much more
stringent than in the frictionless case. Finally, Shimer (2001), for a market
model with coordination friction, obtains a positive correlation between
worker and employer productive ability in equilibrium given sufficient

complementarity, even though in reasonable examples "mismatch" is pervasive in the sense that every employer hires workers of any ability type with positive probability.

More than complementarity in production is required for positive assortative matching, however. The assumption that only pairs are productive plays a crucial role in assignment models. More generally, a capacity constraint is required for an employer with a vacancy to refuse to hire an applicant at a wage less than her marginal product. If production technology exhibits constant returns to scale at the firm level as assumed, there is no reason to deny employment to one worker in hopes of finding another who is more skilled even if worker skill and firm efficiency are complementary provided, of course, that the value of the worker's marginal product is not less than the wage paid.

To illustrate this point, one need only consider two levels of worker skill. Let py represent the productivity of a match composed of an employer of productivity type p and a worker of skill or "human capital" type y. Suppose that y takes on one of two values, y_1 and y_2, where without loss of generality $y_2 > y_1 > 0$. One generally expects that more able workers have higher reservation wages. For simplicity, I assume that a worker's reservation wage is proportional to his skill, that is,

$$b_j = by_j. \tag{1.32}$$

Consider an employer of type p who offers a wage vector $(w_1(p), w_2(p))$ where $w_j(p)$ is the wage offered to applicants of type j. If the employer hires a worker of type j, she earns a profit equal to $py_j - w_j(p)$. Not knowing worker identities ex ante, the employer randomly contacts v workers at a cost $c(v)$. Now, any worker contacted by an employer is offered the appropriate type contingent wage and accepts it only if it is the highest among the offers received. Hence, the probability that a type j worker accepts an offer of w is $P(F_j(w), \lambda)$ as defined in equation (1.7) where now $F_j(w)$ is the distribution of wages offered to workers of type j.

Given constant returns in production, the employer will hire any number of both types contacted who are willing to accept the offer provided, of course, that match productivity exceeds the wage paid. Hence, the employer's total expect profit is

$$\Pi(p) = \max_{(v, w_1, w_2) \geq (0, b_1, b_2)} \{v[q\pi_1(p, w_1)\theta_1(p, w)$$

$$+ (1 - q)\pi_2(p, w_2)\theta_2(p, w)] - c(v)\}, \tag{1.33}$$

where here q represents the fraction of low-skill workers in the labor force,

$$\pi_j(p, w) = P(F_j(w), \lambda)(py_j - w) \tag{1.34}$$

is expected profit per worker contacted of type j contingent on employer productivity and wage offer, and the optimal employment decision is

$$\theta_j(p, w) = \begin{cases} 1 & \text{if } py_j > w_j \\ \in [0, 1] & \text{if } py_j = w_j \\ 0 & \text{if } py_j < w_j \end{cases} \tag{1.35}$$

As a corollary of (1.33), (1.34), and (1.35),

$$w_1(p) = \arg\max_{w \geq b_1} \pi_1(p, w) \quad \text{if } \theta_1(p, w) = 1,$$

$$w_2(p) = \arg\max_{w \geq b_2} \pi_2(p, w) \quad \text{if } \theta_2(p, w) = 1,$$

and

$$c'(v(p)) = \pi^*(p) = q \max_{w \geq b_1} \pi_1(p, w)\theta_1(p, w)$$

$$+ (1 - q) \max_{w \geq b_2} \pi_2(p, w)\theta_2(p, w) \tag{1.36}$$

define an optimal wage and recruiting policy for any employer of type p.

Now, since the expected profit per worker contacted given an offer w less than or equal to the lowest alternative offer in the market for either worker type, $\pi_j(p, w) = P(0, \lambda)(py_j - w)$, is strictly decreasing in w, the lower support of the set of optimal wage policies given that the firm wants to employ the worker is $\underline{w}_j = b_j = by_j$. Hence, the equal profit condition

$$\pi_j(p, w_j(p)) = P(F_j(w_j(p)), \lambda)(py_j - w_j(p)) = P(0, \lambda)(p - b)y_j > 0$$

implies that any optimal offer $w_j(p)$ yield a strictly positive expected profit per worker of type j contacted for any employer with productivity $p > b$. Since by implication $py_j > w_j(p)$, all workers of type j are hired by such an employer from (1.35) and only these employers participate from (1.36), that is, $v(p) > 0 \Rightarrow py_j > w_j(p) \Rightarrow \theta_j(p) = 1$ for all j. This fact and the assumption that workers are contacted at random imply that each employer hires a random sample of the labor force even though worker and employer contributions to the match product are complementary in the example.

In sum, there is no correlation between worker and employer types across pairs in an equilibrium solution to our model when extended to allow for heterogeneity in worker skills. Because the assumption that there is no capacity constraint on the number of jobs offered by an employer is crucial, the result is at one extreme of a continuum and the assortative matching outcome in a perfectly competitive solution to the assignment problem is at the other. In the mirky middle ground between diminishing returns and search friction lies reality. Whether worker and employer contributions to match productivity are positively correlated is, then, an empirical question. As already noted, preliminary evidence reported by Abowd, Kramarz, and Margolis (1999), Abowd, Finer and Kramarz (1999), and Abowd, Creecy, and Kramarz (2002) for both France and the United States suggests not.

1.4 Summary

I began the chapter by documenting a need for a theory of wage dispersion. The fact that the workhorse of labor economics, the human capital wage equation, explains a relatively small fraction of the variance in wages earned across individual workers provides prima facie evidence for this fact. Large and systematic industry and size differentials add further force to the argument. Although some believe that these differentials are the consequence of differences in employment pay policies, others suggest that they reflect differences in unobserved worker ability across industries and firms of different sizes. Recent efforts to resolve this debate by directly measuring firm effects in wages using matched employee-employer data files have shown that at least half of the industry differential and more than 70 percent of the size differential can be attributed to the fact that firms pay observably identical workers differently.

In the second half of the chapter, I introduce two candidate wage determination models that are consistent with observed dispersion. The first is a model inspired by the work of Butters (1977) and Burdett and Judd (1983) in which each employer chooses a wage policy in imperfect Bertrand competition with other employers. The second embodies the hypothesis that wages are determined as the outcome of bilateral bargaining between worker and employer after they meet as characterized in Pissarides (2000). In both models, the source of wage differences arise because workers have incomplete information about the wages offered by the various employers. Given productive heterogeneity across firms, both models can explain industry and size differentials in principle. Finally, I argued that compensating differentials, efficiency wages, and sorting may well contribute but are unlikely to be either the sole or even the most important explanations for cross-employer differences in wages paid.

Notes

1. This is a variant of what is called the "urn matching model" in the search literature.

2. See Burdett and Judd (1983) and Mortensen (1990) for more detailed discussions of these claims.

3. Mortensen (1990) provides a more complete proof and derivation.

2   The Burdett-Mortensen Model

2.1   Introduction

In this chapter, an intertemporal generalization of the one-period model is studied. In what has become known as the Burdett-Mortensen model introduced by Mortensen (1990) and extended in Burdett and Mortensen (1998), workers seek better paying jobs while employed as well as when unemployed. Because time is required to generate offers, on the one hand, and because a new flow of workers continuously enters the state of unemployment, on the other, low- and high-wage employers can coexist.

As in the one-period model, an equilibrium solution to a wage setting game played by identical workers and employers is one in which employers offer different wage rates but all earn the same profit. The unique market equilibrium in this environment is fully characterized. In this chapter, employers are equally productive. Heterogeneity in productive efficiency is introduced in chapter 3.

The model introduced in chapter 1 is a natural starting point for a theory of wage dispersion. In the model, the specific terms of any particular job offer, summarized by the wage, are not known to the worker ex ante. This information is communicated imperfectly by employers, say by posting a notice on <www.monster.com>. Information is incomplete in the sense that each worker observes only a subsample of these notices in any finite interval of time. Because there is only a single time period in the simple model, no time is available for searching for the best employment opportunity available.

Allowing for more than a single period is the principal theoretical development presented in this chapter. In this richer world, workers flow over time into and out of employment and between jobs while employed. Workers who failed to receive a job offer were not employed in the one-period model. In the dynamic generalization, every moment is followed by another. Hence, a worker has an incentive to shop for jobs by both refusing to accept those that offer unattractive terms of employment when unemployed and by seeking a better terms while employed. In other words, they have the opportunity to find the best job over time. Still, so long as the process of matching worker and job is costly and time consuming and jobs are not permanent, differences in wage policies exist.

2.2 Wage Policy and Reservation Wage

Now, suppose the future is represented by an infinite sequence of discrete periods each of length Δ. In this world, some workers are unemployed while others are employed at the beginning of each period. Each of the unemployed who receive an acceptable offer during the period become employed. Those already employed seek a better job and quit when one is found. Hence, an employer's wage policy must be designed to retain existing employees as well as attract new ones in an intertemporal extension of the model.

Here, I assume that each firm pursues a stationary wage policy, namely, the wage originally offered and accepted continues to be the wage paid throughout the tenure of a particular job-worker match. Of course, there are both theoretical and empirical objections to the assumption that a wage offer is independent of a worker's tenure and experience. For example, a fixed wage policy is generally not time consistent in the sense that an employer has an incentive to renege on any initial offer greater than the worker's reservation wage even if the higher offer was initially required to obtain acceptance. Of course, were he to do so, one might expect some retaliation on the worker's part—say, an instantaneous quit and/or bad-mouthing the employer to other workers, acts that affect the employer's future profit. Hence, employers have an incentive to build a reputation for honesty. Coles (2001) has shown that this motive can sustain a constant wage policy in spite of an employer's temptation to chisel.

As in the one-period model, I suppose that each employer contacts a finite number of workers at random in each period. Any contacted worker is unemployed, then, with probability equal to the unemployment rate, u, and accepts any offer in excess of the reservation wage, denoted R, with probability

$$P(F(w), \lambda\Delta) = \sum_{x=0}^{\infty} F(w)^x \frac{e^{-\lambda\Delta}(\lambda\Delta)^x}{x!} = e^{-\lambda\Delta[1-F(w)]}, \qquad (2.1)$$

where now $\lambda\Delta$ is the expected number of offers received by a worker in a period of length Δ. As derived in equation (1.7) above for the case of $\Delta = 1$, $P(F(w), \lambda\Delta)$ is the probability that the offer w is the highest in the set of offers obtained during the period.

Employment contracts are long-lived in the sense that any terms set initially are in force for as long as both employer and employee continue to abide by them. Of course, a mutual decision to begin an employment relationship implies a willingness to continue the match in the future in the absence of a change in the circumstances of the two parties. Under the assumption that the wage is set at the beginning of a match as a matter of policy, the worker quits when a better offer is received. Hence, if an employed worker obtains an offer w, the worker accepts if and only if w is both the highest outside alternative received and if the offer exceeds the worker's current wage.

In sum, the overall probability that a wage offer $w \geq R$ is accepted by a randomly selected worker in the multiperiod model is the following increasing function of the wage offered

$$h(w) = [u + (1 - u)G(w)] P(F(w), \lambda\Delta),$$

where u, the unemployment rate, represents the probability that the worker selected is unemployed and $G(w)$ is the fraction of employed workers who earn a wage less than w. The product of the acceptance probability and the expected present value of the future profit associated with hiring a worker represents the total value of offering a job. In other words, the expected profit per worker contacted can be written as $\pi(p, w, F(w)) = h(w)J(p, w)$ where $J(p, w)$ is the value of hiring a worker at wage w.

To derive the functional form of $J(p, w)$, one must account explicitly for the possibility that the worker once hired may quit as well as the probability of job destruction. The worker quits in any future period if the wage earned, w, is less than the best of the x other offers received during the period. Because the probability of staying is equal to the probability that all outside offers are less than w, which is $F(w)^x$ given that x other offers are received, and because number of other offers received in a period of length Δ is Poisson with expectation $\lambda\Delta$, the quit probability is

$$Q(F(w), \lambda\Delta) = \sum_{x=0}^{\infty} [1 - F(w)^x] \frac{e^{-\lambda\Delta}(\lambda\Delta)^x}{x!} = 1 - P(F(w), \lambda\Delta)$$

after substituting appropriately from equation (2.1). In other words, the probability that a worker quits a job paying w is equal to the probability that the worker's current wage is not the highest offer available.

Since the employer earns the difference between the value of the product of the match p and the wage paid w in each future period so long as the relationship lasts, the expected present value of hiring a worker can be computed using the recursive equation

$$(1 + r\Delta) J(p, w) = (p - w)\Delta + [1 - \delta\Delta - Q(F(w), \lambda\Delta)] J(p, w),$$

where r is the interest rate and δ represents an exogenous job destruction rate. Hence, the value of hiring a worker is simply the discounted cash flow $p - w$ per period where the discount rate equals the sum of the interest rate and match separation rate, that is,

$$J(p, w) = \frac{p - w}{r + \delta + Q(F(w), \lambda\Delta)/\Delta}.$$

Burdett and Mortensen (1998) assume a sequential search conducted in continuous time. In that context, both the acceptance probability, $h(w)$, and the value of hiring a worker, $J(p, w)$, are the limits of the expressions given earlier as the length of the period, Δ, tends to zero. Formally,

$$h(w) = \lim_{\Delta\to 0} [u + (1 - u)G(w)]e^{-\lambda\Delta[1 - F(w)]} = u + (1 - u)G(w) \qquad (2.2)$$

and

$$J(p, w) = \lim_{\Delta\to 0} \frac{p - w}{r + \delta + (1 - e^{-\lambda\Delta[1 - F(w)]})/\Delta}$$

$$= \frac{p - w}{r + \delta + \lambda[1 - F(w)]}, \qquad (2.3)$$

where $\lambda[1 - F(w)]$, the product of the offer arrival rate and the probability that an outside offer exceeds a worker's current wage, is the continuous time quit rate. The fact that all unemployed workers accept any wage above their common reservation level is the simplification obtained by setting the problem in continuous time.

Finally, the expected profit per worker contacted is the product of the probability that the worker accepts and the value of the worker to the firm once employed, that is,

$$\pi(p, w) = h(w)J(p, w) = \frac{(u + (1-u)G(w))(p - w)}{r + \delta + \lambda[1 - F(w)]}.$$ (2.4)

Of course, an optimal wage choice is defined by

$$w = \arg\max_{w \geq R} \pi(p, w).$$ (2.5)

An employer's optimal wage choice in the intertemporal model balances the fact that a higher wage decreases net earning per worker employed but increases the probabilities of both an initial acceptance and retention in the future. Of course, each employer makes this decision in a noncooperative context in which the other employers' wage policies, represented now by both the offer distribution $F(w)$ and the distribution of wages earned by employed worker $G(w)$, are taken as given.

The reservation wage R in the intertemporal model equates the value of employment, $W(w)$, with the value of unemployment, denoted U. In continuous time, the expected present value of employment satisfies the recursive equations

$$(1 + r)W(w) = w + \delta U + \lambda \int \max \langle W(x), W(w) \rangle \, dF(x),$$

given a layoff rate of δ and an offer arrival rate of λ. Under the assumption that the offer arrival rate is the same whether employed or not, the value of unemployment solves the analogous equation

$$(1 + r)U = b + \lambda \int \max \langle W(x), W(w) \rangle \, dF(x).$$

The reservation wage, the solution to $W(R) = U$, is simply

$$R = b$$ (2.6)

as in the one-period model.[1]

2.3   Steady-State Search Equilibrium

Both the unemployment rate in the labor market under study, u, and the wage c.d.f., $G(w)$, evolve over time in response to worker flows among employment states and employers. Although the wage policies chosen for each cohort of job offers may generally be contingent on these aggregate state variables, our interest is in the distribution of wages paid that prevails after a dynamic adjustment to a market steady state. The laws of motion are defined in this section as well as the market solution concept of interest.

In the case of identical workers, each requiring the same reservation wage denoted as $R = b$, all wage offers made are acceptable to the unemployed in any equilibrium. Hence, unemployed workers find a job at the offer arrival rate λ. Because workers who voluntarily quit only do so to accept another job, the transition rate from employment to unemployment is equal to the job destruction rate δ. Given the assumption that the labor force is a continuum represented by the unit interval, the fraction of unemployed evolves according to the simple deterministic rule

$$\dot{u} = \delta(1 - u) - \lambda u,$$

where $\dot{u}$ represents the time rate of change.

A similar argument can be used to derive the change in the fraction of workers who are employed and earn a wage equal to w or less. Let $E(w) = (1 - u)G(w)$ represent this number. The flow into the specified stock is equal to the number of unemployed workers who find employment at a wage less than or equal to w and the flow out is the number of workers employed at wage w or less who either transit to unemployment as a consequence of job destruction or who find an alternative job that pays more than w. Formally,

$$\dot{E}(w) = \lambda F(w)u - (\delta + \lambda[1 - F(w)]) E(w).$$

As one can easily verify, every solution to this system of linear differential equations converges over time to the unique steady state characterized by

$$\frac{u}{1 - u} = \frac{\delta}{\lambda} \qquad\qquad\qquad (2.7)$$

and

$$G(w) \equiv \frac{E(w)}{1 - u} = \left(\frac{\lambda F(w)}{\delta + \lambda[1 - F(w)]}\right)\left(\frac{u}{1 - u}\right) = \frac{\delta F(w)}{\delta + \lambda[1 - F(w)]},$$

$$\qquad\qquad\qquad (2.8)$$

where the last equality is an implication of (2.7).

A steady-state equilibrium solution to the model is a contact frequency λ, a wage offer c.d.f. $F(w)$, an unemployment rate u, and a distribution of wages $G(w)$ that satisfy these steady state conditions, the requirement that every wage offered maximizes expected profit per worker contacted, and a free entry condition. For the same reasons given in the one-period model, the only candidate for an equilibrium offer distribution is a continuous function defined on a connected interval with lower support equal to the common reservation wage b. Because employers are identical, all the offers must yield the same expected profit. After substitution from the steady-state equations into equation (2.4), the equal profit condition implies

$$\pi(p, b) = \left(\frac{\delta}{\delta + \lambda}\right)\left(\frac{p - b}{r + \delta + \lambda}\right) =$$

$$\pi(p, w) = \left(\frac{\delta}{\delta + \lambda[1 - F(w)]}\right)\left(\frac{p - w}{r + \delta + \lambda[1 - F(w)]}\right). \tag{2.9}$$

Since the last term on the right is strictly increasing in $F(w)$ and is decreasing in w while the first term is independent of both, a unique solution for an equilibrium offer distribution exists given any positive finite value for the frequency with which firms contact workers λ.

As in the previous chapter, it is useful to think of the contact frequency λ as determined by employer recruiting behavior. In the simplest case, the cost of contacting a worker is a constant denoted by c. Since expected return per worker contacted is $\pi(p, w)$, which is equal to $\pi(p, b)$ in equilibrium by the equal profit condition, the only aggregate contact frequency consistent with optimality is given by the "free entry" condition

$$\pi(p, b) = \left(\frac{\delta}{\delta + \lambda}\right)\left(\frac{p - b}{r + \delta + \lambda}\right) = c. \tag{2.10}$$

Obviously, equation (2.10) has a unique positive solution if and only if $(p - b)/(r + \delta) > c$. Given the solution, equation (2.9) can be used to solve for the unique equilibrium offer distribution. The associated equilibrium unemployment rate and distribution of wages earned by employed workers are those defined by equations (2.7) and (2.8).

2.4   Equilibrium Wage Dispersion

Equation (2.9) defines a quadratic equation in the offer c.d.f. $F(w)$. The root of interest is

$$F(w) = \frac{r + 2(\delta + \lambda)}{2\lambda} \left[1 - \sqrt{\frac{r^2 + 4(\delta + \lambda)(r + \delta + \lambda)\left(\frac{p-w}{p-b}\right)}{[r + 2(\delta + \lambda)]^2}} \right]. \quad (2.11)$$

This solution limits to the Burdett-Mortensen equilibrium distribution as the interest rate tends to zero.[2] Indeed, the offer and wage distributions respectively converge to

$$F(w) = \frac{\delta + \lambda}{\lambda} \left[1 - \sqrt{\left(\frac{p-w}{p-b}\right)} \right] \quad (2.12)$$

and

$$G(w) = \frac{\delta F(w)}{\delta + \lambda[1 - F(w)]} = \frac{\delta}{\lambda} \left[\sqrt{\left(\frac{p-b}{p-w}\right)} - 1 \right] \quad (2.13)$$

as the interest rate r vanishes. Equation (2.12) and $F(\overline{w}) = 1$ imply that the upper support, the largest wage paid denoted as $\overline{w}$, is determined by

$$\overline{w} = \left[1 - \left(\frac{\delta}{\delta + \lambda}\right)^2 \right] p + \left(\frac{\delta}{\delta + \lambda}\right)^2 b. \quad (2.14)$$

In other words, the highest wage in the market is a weighted average of match productivity and the reservation wage where the weight on the latter is the square of the unemployment rate. As the riskless rate of return is small relative to the sum of the job destruction rate and offer arrival rate estimated from data, the right sides of (2.12) and (2.13) should be good empirical approximation. Because the various expressions are simpler when $r = 0$ and the qualitative implications are the same for all $r > 0$, I often focus on this special case in the rest of this book.

The ratio of the job destruction rate, δ, to the rate at which workers receive offers, the aggregate contact rate per worker λ, has become known as the *market friction parameter* in the literature. From equation (2.7), its value determines the steady-state unemployment rate in the model. Market friction is also an important determinant of both the location and spread of the equilibrium wage and offer distributions. Both the probability of receiving a higher offer, $1 - F(w)$, and of earning a higher wage, $1 - G(w)$, decrease with market friction. In addition, wage dispersion disappears in the following sense as market friction vanishes. Namely, because $\overline{w} \to p$ as $\delta/\lambda \to 0$ from (2.14) while $G(w) \to 0$ for all

$w < \overline{w}$ from (2.13) and $u \to 0$ from (2.7), it follows that all employed workers earn their marginal product, and no one is unemployed in the limit as market friction vanishes. In the absence of friction then, steady state labor market search equilibrium has all the properties of perfect competition.

The market friction parameter also determines the extent to which the offer distribution and the steady-state distribution of earnings across employed workers differ. Indeed, because (2.8) can be rewritten as

$$\frac{F(w) - G(w)}{(1 - F(w))\, G(w)} = \frac{\lambda}{\delta}, \tag{2.15}$$

employed workers are more likely to earn a wage in excess of that offered a new employee in the sense that $G(w)$ stochastically dominates $F(w)$. Indeed, the difference between the two distributions, measured, say, by the difference in medians, increases as the friction parameter decreases.

What determines the extent of friction in a labor market? A related literature reviewed by Mortensen and Pissarides (1999a,b) and integrated by Pissarides (2000) explores this question in some detail. Although wages in these models are determined by bilateral bargaining, the essential explanations of how the offer arrival rate and the job destruction rate are determined can be imported into the Burdett-Mortensen framework as pointed out in Mortensen (2000).

The contact frequency λ depends on the employers' collective willingness to recruit workers. Indeed, if we suppose that the aggregate contact frequency increases so long as the net profit attributable to contacting the marginal worker is positive and that the cost per contact is a constant c, then free entry will drive the common profit per contact, π, down to the cost of making a contact, c, as stated in equation (2.10). In other words, λ is determined by the free entry condition (when for simplicity $r = 0$)

$$\pi(p, w) = \frac{\delta(p - w)}{(\delta + \lambda[1 - F(w)])^2} = c \quad \forall w \in [b, \overline{w}] \tag{2.16}$$

given the wage offer distribution.

Since profits are equal for all wage offers in the support of the equilibrium wage offer distribution, the unique equilibrium value of the offer arrival rate, λ, solves

$$\frac{\delta(p - b)}{(\delta + \lambda)^2} = c$$

from equation (2.16). The solution of interest for the inverse of the friction parameter,

$$\frac{\lambda}{\delta} = \sqrt{\frac{p-b}{\delta c}} - 1, \tag{2.17}$$

is positive if and only if the net output of a job-worker match exceeds the amortized cost of contacting a worker, namely, $p - b > \delta c$. When positive, the equilibrium offer arrival rate is increasing in the difference between market productivity and the reservation wage and is decreasing in the cost of contacting a worker. Although, λ can increase with the job destruction rate over some range, the ratio λ/δ is generally decreasing in δ. Hence, the market friction parameter, δ/λ, is increasing in the job destruction rate δ and the cost of contacting a worker c and is decreasing in net market productivity, $p - b$. Furthermore, market friction vanishes as the cost of contact falls to zero in the sense that $\delta/\lambda \to 0$ as $c \to 0$. In that sense, friction is the cost of contacting workers in this model.

As suggested by the terminology, a large component of the labor turnover represents job destruction. Although the job destruction rate is modeled here by an exogenous parameter, δ, it too can be regarded as an outcome of employer decisions to continue or not continue a particular productive activity in response to shocks to tastes or technology. Eventually, every job match dies in response to some shock that has a sufficiently adverse impact on future profitability. I abstract from these complications in order to focus more clearly on the process of job-worker matching and wage determination even though a combined analysis provides a richer understanding of worker flows. The interested reader is referred to Mortensen and Pissarides (1994) for an analysis of these issues.

2.5 Summary

In this chapter, the Burdett-Mortensen continuous time dynamic labor market model with homogenous agents is presented and studied. The market is composed of two sets of agents, workers and employers. In the market, workers are either employed or unemployed at any point in time. A particular worker transits from unemployment to employment at a rate that depends on the aggregate number of worker contacts made by employers. The transition rate from employment to unemployment is an exogenous job destruction frequency. Employers inform workers of their wage policy by contacting them sequentially at random. Any worker contacted by an employer decides whether or not to accept the job offered. If the worker contacted is unemployed, acceptance implies a transit to employment while it implies a transit from one job to another without an unemployment spell if the worker is employed.

All the agents of each type are identical in the sense that the output of any worker-employer match is the same and each agent acts to maximize the expected present value of her own future income using the same discount factor. Each employer posts a permanent wage that is optimal in this class, given the wages offered by all other employers and the acceptance and search effort strategy pursued by the representative worker. Each worker adopts an acceptance and search effort strategy that maximizes the expected discounted value of future earnings net of search costs. The aggregate number of offers made per time period is determined by free entry. A labor market equilibrium is an aggregate flow of worker contacts that satisfies the free entry condition and an offer distribution function with the property that every wage in its support yields the same expected profit per worker contacted. The unique equilibrium solution to the model is derived in the chapter. Interestingly, the equilibrium distribution can be expressed as a closed form function of model parameters.

Notes

1. In the original Burdett and Mortensen (1998) paper and related literature, the offer arrival rate when unemployed is usually allowed to differ from the arrival rate when employed for empirical reasons. I abstract from this case for simplicity here.

2. Burdett and Mortensen and much of the subsequent literature assume that the wage choice maximizes an employer's average profit over the long run rather than the value of offering a new job. As Mortensen (2000) notes, this criterion is justified only if the employers do not discount the future, namely, $r = 0$. In this limiting case, the two criteria are equivalent.

3

The Shape of Wage Dispersion

The implications of the Burdett-Mortensen model and its extensions for the extent and shape of cross-firm wage dispersion are derived in this chapter. I begin by documenting the shapes of the cross-firm distributions of average wages offered and paid by employers in Danish data. The employment weighted distribution of average wages paid by privately owned Danish firms is well approximated by the lognormal distribution. The job offer weighted distribution of average firm wages is even more skewed as well as stochastically dominated by the distribution of wages paid.

The fact that the Burdett-Mortensen theory of pure dispersion cannot explain these shapes is well known. The same theory extended to allow for productive heterogeneity across employers is shown to be more promising. Two variations of the model with productive heterogeneity are studied. In the first, productivity differences across employers are exogenous, but in the second productivity differences are equilibrium outcomes generated by the incentives implicit in joint wage policy and capital investment decisions.

3.1 The Wage and Offer Distributions

Any interesting theory of wage dispersion must be able to explain the shape of as well as the extent of the dispersion in the distribution of wages paid across firms. But what are these properties? Unlike the distribution of wages earned across workers, little is known about the shape of the cross-firm distribution of wages paid in part because comprehensive wage data at the firm level has only recently become available.

Recently, a group of colleagues and I (see Christiansen et al. (2001)) have been studying the relationship between average wages paid by private-sector firms and worker flows in and out of these firms founded in Danish data. In Christensen et al. (2001), Danish wage data is drawn from the Integrated Database for Labor Market Research (IDA) for the year between November 1994 and November 1995 to construct employment weighted distributions of wages paid by Danish employers.[1] First, the average hourly wage paid during the year by each of the 113,325 private employers is considered. Second, the average wage paid and the number of workers employed by each firm are used to construct the employment weighted distribution of wages paid across employers. The empirical counterpart of the wage density computed for the full sample, $g(w) = G'(w)$, is plotted in figure 3.1. Obviously, the distribution is skewed with a long right tail. Indeed, the lognormal density with same log wage mean and variance, represented in the figure by the dashed curve, approximates the general shape of the wage density quite well. This result contrasts with the shapes found for distributions of earning that typically have a longer and fatter right tail, one that is better approximated by the Pareto distribution.[2]

Christensen et al. (2001) construct the associated distribution of wages offered during the November 1994–November 1995 year by weighting the average wage paid by each firm by the number of workers hired from

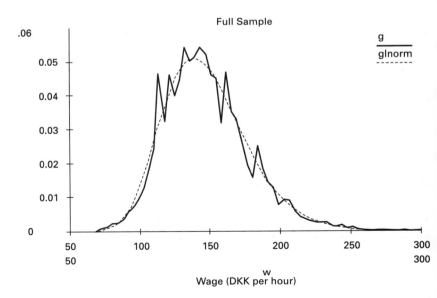

Figure 3.1
Actual (g) and lognormal ($glnorm$) wage densities.

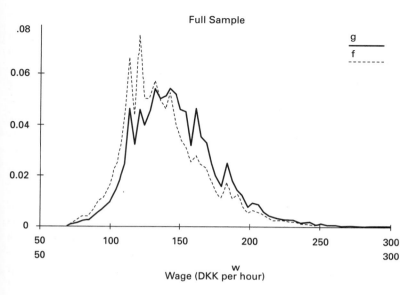

Figure 3.2
Offer (f) and wage (g) densities.

unemployment during the year. Workers hired from employment are excluded in the construction because this subsample is biased upward to the extent that the employed only move from lower to higher paying firms as predicted by the Burdett-Mortensen model. The resulting wage offer distribution density function, $f(w)$, is illustrated by the dotted curve figure 3.2. Again, the wage density, $g(w)$, is plotted as a solid curve. Although a smoothed version of the empirical offer distribution is also unimodal, it is more skewed right than the wage density. Also, note that the observed distribution of wages paid stochastically dominates the wage offer distribution as equation (2.8) requires.

If all workers were identical, as in our hypothetical environment, the observed variation in average wages paid would reflect only wage dispersion induced by differences in employer pay policies. Of course, workers are not equally able in reality. Now, it is conceivable that this fact alone provides an explanation for the observed skew in the distribution of wages paid in Denmark.

The theory of occupation selection as described by the Roy (1950, 1951) model is one explanation for the observed skew in the distribution of worker earnings. In that formulation, the returns to worker ability differ across occupations, but workers choose to work in the job that maximizes earnings given ability. Formally, suppose that

$$w_{ij} = \alpha_i + \beta_i y_j,\tag{3.1}$$

where w_{ij} represent the wage paid worker j in occupation i (his productivity in the occupation in the Roy model), y_j is some measure of the general ability of worker j, and α_i and β_i are coefficients that characterized the (linear) relationship between ability and productivity in occupation i. However, the actual wage observed for individual i given his optimal occupation choice is

$$w(y) = \max_i \langle \alpha_i + \beta_i y \rangle.\tag{3.2}$$

As the maximum of a set of linear functions with different slopes in convex, the observed distribution of wages earned by a set of individuals has a long right tail even if the distribution of worker ability were symmetric.

Although the Roy model may well capture the wage distribution consequences of occupation choice, this fact need not explain the observed shape of the employment weighted distribution of average wages paid. For example, if each firm offers a wage composed of a worker-specific component reflecting known ability plus its own employer fixed effect, and if output is linear in the number of workers employed in each occupation, then our model implies no correlation between worker and employer fixed effects. As demonstrated in chapter 1, every employer's labor force is a random sample of the population. Furthermore, the low correlations between worker and employer fixed effects estimated from similar matched data reported by Abowd, Kramarz, and their colleagues is consistent with this hypothesis. Although the Abowd-Kramarz decomposition of the log wages found in the IDA has not been performed, these data are available by occupation. This fact provides a test of the independence assumption, at least to the extent that occupation status reflects worker ability as suggested by the Roy model.

The Danish IDA identifies the job of each employee as belonging to one of the following mutually exclusive occupational categories: managers, salaried workers, skilled workers, and unskilled workers. According to the Roy model, these categories should be proxies for worker ability. The actual wage and the lognormal densities for each occupation category are illustrated in the panels of figure 3.3. Although the lognormal fits less well for some occupations, especially for managers, measures of dispersion, the general shapes, and particularly the tail properties of the wage densities are similar across the four cases.

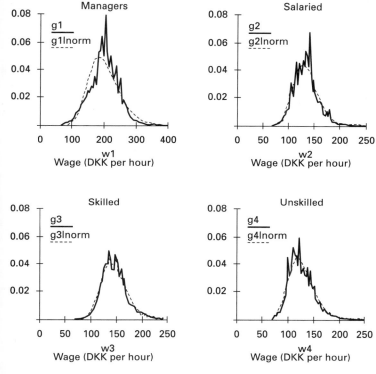

Figure 3.3
Actual (g) and lognormal wage ($glnorm$) densities by occupation.

The means and standard deviations of log wage as well as the log wage at the 10th and 90th percentile are reported for the full sample as well as each subsample in table 3.1.

As illustrated in figure 3.3, the Roy model specification and the assumption that employers differ with respect to the occupation composition of their labor forces imply that within occupation, dispersion is much less than the dispersion of the full sample. Indeed, in the extreme case in which all employees of each firm are of the same occupation, the ranges of the distributions are necessarily disjoint. In contrast, the variances of all four distributions reported table 3.1 are quite similar in magnitude to both one another and to the variance of the pooled sample. Similarly, the ratios of the 90th percentile to the 10th percentile of each distribution are also close in value. For the full sample, the 90-10 log wage ratio is 1.111, while for the four subsamples in the same

Table 3.1
Danish IDA wage and offer distribution statistics

	Full sample	Managers	Salaried	Skilled	Unskilled
Mean log wage	4.972	5.273	4.878	4.959	4.822
Std. dev. log wage	0.204	0.238	0.177	0.170	0.197
10th percentile	4.710	4.883	4.585	4.682	4.500
90th percentile	5.231	5.580	5.106	5.176	5.075
No. of firms	113,325	49,667	57,513	44,527	70,886
Employment share	1.0000	0.2075	0.2410	0.1782	0.3731

order, the ratios equal 1.143, 1.114, 1.106, 1.128. Finally, the ranges between the 10th and the 90th percentile have substantial overlap, and the cross-firm variation swamps the cross-occupation variation in the log wage. Although the means generally increase with ability as reflected in occupation status, these properties of the observed wage dispersion suggest that occupation self-selection is not an important explanation for the shape of the cross-firm distribution of average wages paid.

As these observations suggest, the distributions of the cross-firm occupation wages paid can be used to test more formally for independence of the worker and employer fixed effects in the wage equation. Suppose that

$$\ln w_{ij} = x_i + y_j, \tag{3.3}$$

where w_{ij} represents the wage earned by a worker of type j when employed by firm i, x_i is the employer fixed effect, and y_j is the fixed effect of worker j. It follows that the average log wage paid by firm i is

$$\overline{\ln w_i} = x_i + \bar{y}_i, \ \bar{y}_i = \frac{1}{n_i} \sum_{j \in I_i} y_j, \tag{3.4}$$

where I_i represents the set of worker indices representing the employees of firm i, n_i is the number of workers so employed, and $\bar{y}_i$ is the sample average of its employees' worker fixed effects. In other words, the average log wage paid is the employer's fixed effect plus the average of her employees' fixed effects. If the set I_i is a random sample of all workers, equivalently x and y are independent across worker-employer pairs, then the employee contribution to the average wage paid is the same in expectation across all firms. Hence, the difference in the average log wage of any two firms equals the difference in employer fixed effect plus "noise."

Of course, the variance of the distribution of average log wages paid across employers is given by

$$Var(\overline{\ln w}) = \sum_i (\ln \overline{w}_i - \mu)^2 \frac{n_i}{n} = \sum_i [x_i - \mu_x + \overline{y}_i - \mu_y]^2 \frac{n_i}{n}$$

$$= \sum_i (x_i - \mu_x)^2 \frac{n_i}{n} + 2 \sum_i (x_i - \mu_x)(\overline{y}_i - \mu_y) \frac{n_i}{n}$$

$$+ \sum_i (\overline{y}_i - \mu_y)^2 \frac{n_i}{n}$$

$$= \sigma_x^2 + 2\sigma_{x\overline{y}} + \sigma_{\overline{y}}^2, \tag{3.5}$$

where σ_x^2, $\sigma_{\overline{y}}^2$, and $\sigma_{x\overline{y}}$ are the variance of x, the variance of $\overline{y}$, and their covariance respectively, $\mu = \mu_x + \mu_y$ is the overall mean and

$$\mu_x = \sum_i x_i \frac{n_i}{n},$$

$$\mu_{\overline{y}} = \sum_i \overline{y}_i \frac{n_i}{n} = \frac{1}{n} \sum_i y_i = \mu_y,$$

and n is the total number of employed workers in the population. The conditional mean and variance of the wage paid to workers of type y are

$$\mu_x(y) = E(\overline{\ln w}|y_j = y) = y + \sum_i \frac{x_i n_i(y)}{n(y)}$$

and

$$\sigma_x^2(y) = Var(\overline{\ln w}|y_j = y) = \sum_i^m (x_i - \mu_x(y))^2 \frac{n_i(y)}{n(y)},$$

where $n_i(y)$ is the number of workers of type y employed by firm i,

$$\sum_y n_i(y) = n_i, \quad \text{and} \quad \sum_i n_i(y) = n(y).$$

It follows that

$$\sum_y Var(\overline{\ln w}|y_j = y) \frac{n(y)}{n} = \sum_y \sigma_x^2(y) \frac{n_i(y)}{n} \tag{3.6}$$

is equal to σ_x^2 if x and y are uncorrelated across worker-employer pairs. Finally,

$$\sum_y (E(\overline{\ln w}|y_j = y) - \mu)^2 \frac{n(y)}{n} = \sum_y (y - \mu_y)^2 \frac{n(y)}{n} = \sigma_y^2. \tag{3.7}$$

Collectively, then, equations (3.5) to (3.6) imply that

$$\sum_y Var(\overline{\ln w}|y_j = y)\frac{n(y)}{n} = \sigma_x^2 = Var(\overline{\ln w}) - \frac{m}{n}\sigma_y^2 \tag{3.8}$$

holds under the hypothesis that x and y are independent across worker-employer pairs and the number of workers and employers, n and m, are both large. Formally, $\sigma_{x\bar{y}} = 0$, $\sigma_x^2(y) = \sigma_x^2$ for all y, and

$$\sigma_{\bar{y}}^2 = \sum_i (\bar{y}_i - \mu_y)^2 \frac{n_i}{n} = \frac{1}{n}\sum_i \left(\frac{\sigma_y^2}{n_i}\right) n_i = \frac{m}{n}\sigma_y^2 \tag{3.9}$$

holds approximately when there are a large number of firms of each size because the expectation of $(\bar{y}_i - \mu_y)^2$ is the $Var(\bar{y}_i) = \sigma_y^2/n_i$.

From table 3.1,

$$Var(\overline{\ln w}) = \sigma_x^2 + \frac{m}{n}\sigma_{\bar{y}}^2 = (0.204)^2 = 0.0416$$

given independence. In addition, if one assumes that worker ability is approximately the same for all workers in the same occupation, then

$$\sum_y Var(\overline{\ln w}|y_j = y)\frac{n(y)}{n} = \sigma_x^2$$

$$= \begin{bmatrix} (0.2075)\,(0.238)^2 + (0.2410)\,(0.177)^2 \\ + (0.1782)\,(0.170)^2 + (0.3731)\,(0.197)^2 \end{bmatrix} = 0.0389$$

and

$$\sum_y (E(\overline{\ln w}|y_j = y) - \mu)^2 \frac{n(y)}{n} = \sigma_y^2$$

$$= \begin{bmatrix} (0.2075)\,(5.273 - 4.972)^2 + (0.2410)\,(4.878 - 4.972)^2 \\ + (0.1782)\,(4.959 - 4.972)^2 + (0.3731)\,(4.822 - 4.972)^2 \end{bmatrix} = 0.0294$$

hold as approximations.

Given these numerical implications of the independence assumption and the fact that the average firm size is $n/m = 13.2$, the right side of (3.8) is equal to $0.0416 - 0.0294/13.2 = 0.0394$, which is obviously very close to the magnitude of the left side, 0.0389. As this fact suggests, one can use the computed values of the variances of x and y as approximations for the purpose of computing the correlation coefficient measuring the dependence between the two components of the average wage paid by a firm, x and $\bar{y}$. Indeed, the implied value is

$$\rho = \frac{\sigma_{x\bar{y}}}{\sigma_x \sigma_{\bar{y}}} = \frac{Var(\ln w) - \sigma_x^2 - \sigma_{\bar{y}}^2}{2\sigma_x \sigma_{\bar{y}}} = \frac{0.0394 - 0.0389}{2\sqrt{0.0389}\sqrt{0.0294/13.2}} = 0.0269.$$

Hence, I conclude that there are no important differences in worker ability across Danish firms at least to the extent that it is reflected in differences in occupation composition.

3.2   Homogenous Productivity

It is well known that the simple version of the Burdett-Mortensen model in which all employers are equally productive and all workers search with equal intensity contradicts evidence on the shape of empirical wage paid and on offered densities of the kind illustrated in figure 3.2. Specifically, the model implies that both density functions are increasing and convex in the wage. The closed form solutions for the two density functions are

$$F'(w) = f(w) = \left(\frac{\delta + \lambda}{2\lambda}\right)\left(\frac{p - b}{p - w}\right)^{\frac{1}{2}}$$

$$G'(w) = g(w) = \left(\frac{\delta}{2\lambda}\right)\left(\frac{p - b}{p - w}\right)^{\frac{3}{2}}$$

(3.10)

in the limiting case of $r = 0$ by differentiation of the two cumulative distribution functions given in (2.12).[3]

The increasing convex shapes of the offer and wage densities obviously hold for any value of the market friction parameter from (3.10). These shapes reflect the fact that worker search generates the incentive for most of the identical employers to offer relatively high wages in an environment characterized by friction and productive homogeneity. The fact that even a larger fraction of workers are employed at higher wages is also the consequence of search on the job. These implications of the model clearly contradict the observations portrayed in figure 3.1. The observed densities are not the outcome of a simple wage posting game played by identical employers.

3.3 Exogenous Productive Heterogeneity

As noted earlier, productive heterogeneity helps explain industry and firm effects in the one-period model. Mortensen (1990), Burdett and Mortensen (1998), and Bontemps, Robin, and van den Berg (2000) all point out that the Burdett-Mortensen model has more realistic implications for the shapes of the offer and wage densities once differences in employer productivity are taken into account in the multiperiod model. Given exogenous heterogeneity of this form, expected profit per worker contacted can be represented as $\pi(p, w) = h(w)J(p, w)$, where now p indexes the employer's specific productivity type, $h(w)$ is the probability that a worker contacted at random will accept the wage w, and $J(p, w)$ is the value of employing a worker to a firm of productivity p paying wage w. Of course,

$$J(p, w) = \frac{p - w}{r + d(w)} \tag{3.11}$$

as shown earlier where $d(w)$ denotes the separation rate. In the case of constant search effort, the separation rate is

$$d(w) = \delta + \lambda[1 - F(w)]. \tag{3.12}$$

As the acceptance probability is $h(w) = u + (1-u)G(w)$, the steady state equations (2.7) and (2.8) imply

$$h(w) = \frac{\delta + \lambda G(w)}{\delta + \lambda} = \frac{\delta}{\delta + \lambda[1 - F(w)]}. \tag{3.13}$$

In sum, the expected profit per worker contacted expressed as a function of the firm's productivity and wage is

$$\pi(p, w) = h(w)J(p, w) = \frac{\delta(p - w)}{(\delta + \lambda[1 - F(w)])^2} \tag{3.14}$$

in the limiting case of $r = 0$.

3.3.1 Wage Policy

The monopsonistic wage of an employer with productivity p maximizes $\pi(p, w)$ as defined in equation (3.14), that is,

$$w(p) = \arg\max_{w \geq b} \pi(p, w).$$

Given the form of the expected profit function, one can show that the optimal wage choice conditional on employer productivity must be an increasing function of the productivity parameter using the same argument as that applied to the one-period model. (See the proof to Proposition 2.) In other words, more productive employers offer higher wages in any equilibrium. Under the assumption that productivity is continuously distributed over employers, the equilibrium wage offered by an employer with productivity p, denoted $w(p)$, is one-to-one. As a consequence, the distribution of wage offers reflects the distribution of productivity across employers in the generalization as well as the strategic forces at work in the wage setting game.

The fraction of offers that pay $w(p)$ or less is simply the fraction of offers made by employers with productivity p or less given $w'(p) > 0$,

$$F(w(p)) = \Gamma(p), \tag{3.15}$$

where $\Gamma(p)$ is the proportion of offers made by employers with productivity no greater than p. Now, because the choice of the wage is unique for any p, the wage function $w(p)$ must satisfy the first-order condition for an interior condition, $\partial \pi(p, w)/\partial w = 0$, which can be written as

$$\frac{2\lambda F'(w)\,(p - w)}{\delta + \lambda[1 - F(w)]} = 1 \tag{3.16}$$

in the limiting case of $r = 0$. Using the fact $F'(w(p))w'(p) = \Gamma'(p) = \gamma(p)$ implied by (3.15), it follows the optimal wage relationship between wage and productivity, $w(p)$, solves the ordinary differential equation

$$w'(p) = \frac{2\lambda \Gamma'(p)\,(p - w(p))}{\delta + \lambda[1 - \Gamma(p)]}. \tag{3.17}$$

Because profit is positive for any participating firm, that is, $p > w(p)$, equation (3.17) implies that more productive employers pay higher wages. Because no employer with productivity less than the common reservation wage can offer a worker an acceptable wage, the lower support of the productivity distribution over employers who participate in the market, denoted by $\underline{p}$, is no less than b. The unique solution to (3.17) associated with the boundary condition

$$w(\underline{p}) = b \tag{3.18}$$

and equation (3.15) fully characterizes the equilibrium distribution of wage offers provided, of course, that labor productivity at the most productive firm exceeds the reservation wage, namely, $\bar{p} > b$.

Given the equilibrium wage function $w(p)$, the associated equilibrium offer and wage densities can be written as

$$f(w(p)) = F'(w(p)) = \frac{\Gamma'(p)}{w'(p)} = \frac{\delta + \lambda[1 - \Gamma(p)]}{2\lambda\,(p - w(p))}$$

$$g(w) = G'(w) = \frac{\delta(\delta + \lambda)f(w)}{(\delta + \lambda[1 - F(w)])^2}, \tag{3.19}$$

where the first equation is an implication of (3.17) and the second equation follows from the steady state condition (2.8). As $\Gamma(p)$ is increasing in p, a sufficient condition for a declining offer wage density is that ex-post profit per worker $p - w(p)$ increases with p from equation (3.19). Because equation (3.17) requires $w'(\bar{p}) = 0$ if $\Gamma'(\bar{p}) = 0$, where $\bar{p}$ is the upper support of the productivity distribution, any continuous productivity distribution with a vanishing right tail does generate an offer distribution with a declining density for all large enough wage rates. Still, the fact that the equilibrium distributions are convex and increasing in the case of a degenerate productivity distribution suggests that a highly skewed distribution of productivity is generally required to generate offer and wage densities with the shape properties of those actually observed.

The wage function and equilibrium offer and wage densities implied by equations (3.17) and (3.19) when $\delta = 0.287$, the estimate of this separation parameter obtained by Christensen et al. (2001), $\lambda = 0.207$, the average of their estimates of the arrival rates over the distribution of wages paid, a reservation wage $b = 0$, and a Pareto distribution of productivity, given by

$$\Gamma(x) = 1 - x^{-a}, \tag{3.20}$$

with shape parameter $a = 2$ are illustrated in figure 3.4. As is well known, the Pareto distribution is declining throughout its support and has a long right tail. The wage offer density would also be Pareto if the wage function $w(p)$ were linear. Instead, the computed theoretical

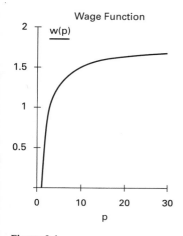
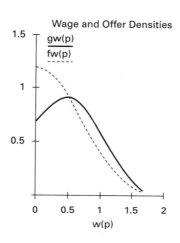

Figure 3.4
Heterogenous productivity I.

wage function, $w(p)$, is highly concave. Although decreasing, the right tails of both the wage and offer densities are short and truncated as a consequence. Still, the computed wage density does have an interior mode even though the density of productivity used to generate it takes on its maximum value at the left support.

Because an employer's quit rate decreases with the wage paid and higher-paid employed workers find it harder to locate a better job, the elasticity of a firm's labor supply decreases as the wage increase. As a consequence, wages in the upper portion of the support of the wage and offer distributions increase less rapidly with employer productivity. The wage and offer densities have short right tails relative to the productivity density as a result. In sum, both wage competition and a skewed distribution of productive heterogeneity with a long right tail are needed to generate the observed shape of wage dispersion.

3.3.2 Recruiting Policy

To maintain dispersion in firm productivity, one cannot close the model by supposing that the aggregate contact rate is determined by setting the return per worker contacted to a constant marginal cost per contact for the following reason. If in fact the marginal cost of recruiting were constant, then only the most productive firms would invest in recruiting in equilibrium as noted in chapter 1. Formally, the only equilibrium possible is one in which the free entry condition, equation (2.16), holds for the most productive employer, that is, $\max_{w \geq b} \{\pi(\bar{p}, w)\} = c$ where c

represents the cost of contacting the marginal worker. As the maximal profit per contact is decreasing in productivity from (3.14), it follows that profit per worker contacted is less than cost for all other employers, $\max_{w \geq b} \{\pi(p, w)\} < c$ for all $p < \bar{p}$. Consequently, only the most productive employers participate in the labor market.

Productivity heterogeneity across firms persists if recruiting costs rise at the margin, however. In this case, more productive firms have an incentive to attract more workers by making more contacts as well as by paying more than less productive employers, but the optimal contact frequency is finite. In addition, the worker separation rates decline with the wage paid. Because more productive firms hire new workers at greater frequency and because those hired stay longer, more productive firms are larger and pay more than less productive firms. In addition, the shapes of the wage and offer densities are modified by the endogeneity of recruiting effort in ways that seem to make them more parsimonious with those actually observed.

To verify these assertions, I extend the model by allowing each employer to choose the number of workers to contact v subject to an increasing and convex cost, $c_f(v)$. In this case, the wage offered and the number of contacts made by a firm of productivity p jointly maximize the total flow of expected profit, namely,

$$(w(p), v(p)) = \arg \max_{(w,v) \geq (b,0)} \{\pi(p, w)v - c_f(v)\}. \tag{3.21}$$

As a corollary, the optimal wage maximizes the expected profit per worker contacted

$$w(p) = \arg \max_{w \geq b} \pi(p, w), \tag{3.22}$$

and the optimal contact frequency of any participating employer of productivity type p is determined by the first-order condition

$$c'(v(p)) = \max_{w \geq b} \pi(p, w). \tag{3.23}$$

By the envelope theorem and the second-order necessary condition for an interior solution, the number of worker contacts made by any employer is an increasing function of the employer's labor productivity, $v'(p) > 0$, because profit per contact increases with p. Furthermore, if the marginal cost is zero at the origin, namely, $c'(0) = 0$, then all employers with labor productivity greater than the reservation wage, $p > b$, offer new jobs in the sense that they make a positive effort to contact potential employees.

Because the number of contacts made varies across employer types in this generalization, the distribution of productivity across jobs offered is now endogenous. Specifically, the wage offer distribution, the vacancy weighted distribution of employer productivity,

$$F(w(p)) = \frac{\int_b^p v(z)\, d\Gamma(z)}{\int_b^{\bar{p}} v(z)\, d\Gamma(z)}, \tag{3.24}$$

replaces (3.15), where here $\Gamma(p)$ represents the distribution of productivity across employers. Given the fact that the number of contacts varies across firm types, the aggregate number of employer contacts per worker in the market is

$$\lambda = m \int_b^{\bar{p}} v(z)\, d\Gamma(z), \tag{3.25}$$

where m is the number of firms per worker in the market. Note that firms with higher productivity represent a larger share of the offers made because $v(p)$ is increasing in p.

A steady state *labor market equilibrium* solution to the model is an offer arrival rate parameter λ and an offer distribution function $F(w)$ that satisfy equations (3.24) and (3.25), given that the wage and recruiting strategies $w(p)$ and $v(p)$ are optimal in the sense of equation (3.21). The first-order condition for an optimal wage policy together with equations (3.23), (3.24), and (3.25) imply

$$w'(p) = \frac{2\,(p - w(p))\,\Gamma'(p)}{\delta + m \int_p^{\bar{p}} v(z)\, d\Gamma(z)},$$

where $\Gamma'(p)$ is the productivity density and the optimal choice of recruiting effort satisfies

$$c'(v(p)) = \frac{\delta(p - w(p))}{\left(\delta + m \int_p^{\bar{p}} v(z)\, d\Gamma(z)\right)^2}.$$

Because the separation hazard expressed as a function of p is

$$q(p) = d(w(p)) = \delta + \lambda[1 - F(w(p))] = \delta + m \int_p^{\bar{p}} v(z)\, d\Gamma(z), \tag{3.26}$$

from equations (3.24) and (3.25), the two equilibrium conditions can be represented as the system of two ordinary differential equations

$$w'(p) = \frac{2(p - w(p))\,\Gamma'(p)}{q(p)} \tag{3.27}$$

and

$$q'(p) = -mv(p)\Gamma'(p) = -m\varphi\left(\frac{\delta(p - w(p))}{q(p)^2}\right)\Gamma'(p), \tag{3.28}$$

where $\varphi(\cdot)$ is the inverse of the marginal cost function $c'_f(v)$.

The unique solution to this ODE system satisfying the two boundary conditions

$$w(\underline{p}) = b \quad \text{and} \quad d(\bar{p}) = \delta \tag{3.29}$$

characterizes the labor market equilibrium solution to the model provided that $\underline{p} \geq b$. As the wage offered can be no less than b, if $\underline{p} < b$, the corner solution $v(p) = 0$ is optimal for all $p \in [\underline{p}, b]$. Hence, $\underline{p} \geq b$ can be assumed without loss of generality provided that the most productive employers participate. In sum, $c(v)$ increasing and strictly convex, $c'(0) = c(0) = 0$, and $\bar{p} > b$ are sufficient conditions for the existence of a unique labor market equilibrium.

The computed wage and vacancy functions, $w(p)$ and $v(p)$, and the offer and wage densities implied by equations (3.27), (3.28), (3.29), (3.24), and (3.25)—given a Pareto distribution of productivity and a quadratic cost of recruiting function with all the other parameters the same as in the previous example, $a = 2$, $\delta = 0.287$, $\lambda = 0.207$, and $b = 0$—are illustrated in figure 3.5. Given the solution to the ODE, the offer p.d.f. was computed using the following implication of the equations:

$$f(w(p))w'(p) = \frac{v(p)\Gamma'(p)}{\int_{\underline{p}}^{\bar{p}} v(z)\,d\Gamma(z)} = \frac{mv(p)\Gamma'(p)}{\lambda} = \frac{-q'(p)}{\lambda}.$$

Finally, the fact that the steady state condition (2.8) implies

$$g(w(p)) = \frac{\delta(\delta + \lambda)f(w(p))}{q(p)^2}$$

was used to compute the wage p.d.f. Note that in the quadratic cost case,

$$mv(p) = \frac{\left(\frac{m}{c_0}\right)\delta(p - w(p))}{\left(\delta + m\int_{\underline{p}}^{\bar{p}} v(z)\,d\Gamma(z)\right)^2},$$

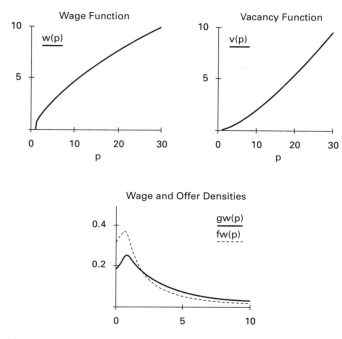

Figure 3.5
Heterogenous productivity II.

where c_0 is the scale parameter of the cost function written as

$$c(v) = \frac{c_0 v^2}{2}.$$

The results are those obtained when the parameter c_0/m is chosen so that the value of λ implied by (3.25) is 0.207.

A comparison of the wage policy curves in figures 3.4 and 3.5 confirms the fact that the wage-productivity relationship is more responsive and less convex when recruiting effort is chosen optimally throughout the wage support. As a result, the offer and wage distributions are unimodal and have longer right tails than those obtained in the constant recruiting effort case. These differences in the features seem to arise because recruiting activity complements wage competition. In other words, given the opportunity to recruit, more productive employers pay more than otherwise as well as invest more in recruiting activity.

Finally, note that the implied shapes of both densities are now similar to those observed for the IDA in figure 3.3. Productive heterogeneity is needed to explain the observed long right tails of both the offer and wage densities. Furthermore, accounting for endogenous recruiting effort improves the ability of the model to mimic the actual shapes of the observed wage and offer distributions.

3.4 Endogenous Productive Heterogeneity

In this section, I show that heterogeneity in employer productivity can be an endogenous consequence of the competitive forces that generate wage dispersion even when all employers are homogenous ex ante. In these models, it is the wage competition alone that induces cross-firm productive heterogeneity. Acemoglu and Shimer (1999) generate endogenous cross-firm dispersion in capital intensity in a one-period model similar to the one-period model introduced in chapter 1. Their logic follows: Suppose all employers are initially identical. Wage dispersion characterizes the only equilibrium in this case. But, given dispersion, a higher-paying employer has an incentive to adopt a more capital-intensive production technology. As a consequence, the workers employed by firms with higher capital labor ratio are more productive. Mortensen (2000) notes that differences in quit rates attributable to wage policy differences generate dispersion in the amounts invested in match-specific capital as well. In both models, causality runs from wage dispersion to productive heterogeneity induced by differences in investment rather than the other way around.

3.4.1 Match-Specific Capital

Let k represent the specific capital an employer invests in a new match, and let $p(k)$ denote the worker's post-investment productivity where the production function $p(k)$ is increasing and concave. Firm-specific training is an example of this form of investment. The expected profit per worker contacted is the product of the probability that a random worker accepts the offer and the difference between the value of employing the worker and the cost of training, namely, $\pi(w) = h(w)[J(p(k), w) - k]$. From equation (3.11), the profit per worker contacted is

$$\pi(w) = \max_{k \geq 0} \left\{ h(w) \left(\frac{p(k) - w}{r + d(w)} - k \right) \right\}.$$ (3.30)

The first-order condition for an optimal choice of training,

$$p'(k(w)) = r + d(w),$$ (3.31)

requires that the optimal investment equates the marginal product with the rate at which income on specific capital is discounted, the sum of the interest rate and the job separation rate. Because the separation rate decreases with the wage paid, higher-paying employers invest more in training, $k'(w) > 0$, by concavity of the production function.

As all employers are identical ex ante, their wage choices must yield the same profit per worker contacted as in the original Burdett-Mortensen model; that is,

$$\pi(w) = h(w) \max_{k \geq 0} \left\{ \frac{p(k) - w}{r + d(w)} - k \right\} = \pi(b) \quad \forall w \in [b, \overline{w}] \tag{3.32}$$

uniquely determines the equilibrium wage offer distribution $F(w)$. Finally, the aggregate number of contacts is the solution to the requirement that the recruiting cost per contact equals the return. Formally,

$$c = \pi(b) = \left(\frac{\delta}{\delta + \lambda} \right) \max_{k \geq 0} \left\{ \frac{p(k) - b}{r + \delta + \lambda} - k \right\}, \tag{3.33}$$

since equations (3.12) and (3.13) imply $h(b) = \frac{\delta}{\delta + \lambda}$ and $d(b) = \delta$. Note that endogenous productive heterogeneity is consistent with a linear recruiting cost because all employers earn the same expected profit per worker contacted. However, if the marginal cost of recruiting were increasing, then all employers contact the same number of workers because expected profit per contact is equal on the support of the equilibrium wage distribution.

In sum, a steady state *labor market equilibrium* is an aggregate contact rate λ that solves the optimal recruiting condition (3.33), a wage offer distribution $F(w)$ that satisfies the equal profit condition (3.32), and the optimal investment strategy $k(w)$ implicitly defined by condition (3.31). Because the right side of (3.33) is strictly decreasing in λ, a unique positive solution exists provided that $p(k) > b$ for some $k \geq 0$. Given the equilibrium value of the contact frequency, the associated unique solution for $F(w)$ and $k(w)$ are implicitly defined by equations (3.32) and (3.31), respectively. The computed equilibrium investment function and the wage and offer densities, given $b = 0$ and a production function of the constant elasticity form $p(k) = k^{\alpha}$ with $\alpha = 0.8$, are illustrated in figure 3.6. The same friction parameters, $\delta = 0.287$ and $\lambda = 0.207$, are assumed. The optimal investment function $k(w)$, offer density $f(w)$, and wage density $g(w)$ are computed as follows. Use the first-order condition (3.31) together with the definitions equations (3.12) and (3.13) to

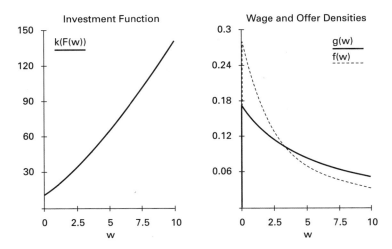

Figure 3.6
Specific capital investment.

solve for $k(w)$ as a function of $F(w)$. After substituting the result and the value of c implied by the right side of (3.33) into (3.32), solve for $F(w)$. Given this offer distribution function, the corresponding steady state wage function $G(w)$ is computed using the steady state condition, equation (2.8). Of course, the density functions plotted in figure 3.6, $f(w)$ and $g(w)$, are the derivatives of the computed functions $F(w)$ and $G(w)$, respectively.

Experimentation suggests that the offer density, $f(w)$, is typically decreasing for all values of α, while the wage density is increasing for lower values and decreasing for higher values. Of course $\alpha = 0$ corresponds to the original homogenous product model. Although some other form for the production function may be needed to match the observed shapes of the wage and offer densities exactly, the example illustrates that decreasing densities can be obtained in the case of identical employers if one allows for investment in match-specific capital.

3.4.2 General Capital
In this case, capital is viewed as embodied in the job rather than the match. In other words, when the job is created, investments are made in the equipment any worker needs to be productive in the job. A personal computer is the obvious example. Unlike the case of match-specific capital, equipment does not vanish if the worker leaves. Instead, the employer can rematch a new worker with the same tool. In this case, the

relative wage paid by an employer is important as a determinant of the utilization rate of the job's equipment. Specifically, capital utilization is higher for employers who pay more because they fill vacant jobs more rapidly and retain workers longer. Since the return to general capital is increasing in the utilization rate, employers who pay more have an incentive to invest more per job created.

Because any job can be rematched with another worker after a quit but is destroyed if the firm shuts down (the scrap value is zero), the value of the job when filled conditional on the wage offered w and the investment made in general capital k solves

$$rJ(p(k), w) = p(k) - w - \delta J(p(k), w)$$

$$+ \lambda(1 - F(w))[V(p(k), w) - J(p(k), w)]. \tag{3.34}$$

The value of the job when vacant, denoted as $V(w, k)$, is determined by the Bellman equation

$$rV(p(k), w) = h(w)[J(p(k), w) - V(p(k), w)] - c - \delta V(p(k), w), \tag{3.35}$$

where $h(w)$ is the acceptance probability and c is the cost of contacting a worker. By subtracting corresponding sides of (3.35) from (3.34), one obtains

$$J(p(k), w) - V(p(k), w) = \frac{p(k) - w + c}{r + d(w) + h(w)}, \tag{3.36}$$

where $d(w) = \delta + \lambda(1 - F(w))$ represents the worker separation rate as previously.

Given the wage offered, the optimal capital investment in a job maximizes its value as a vacancy; that is,

$$\pi(w) = \max_{k \geq 0}(r + \delta)[V(p(k), w) - k]$$

$$= \arg\max_{k \geq 0}\left\{ \frac{[p(k) - w]h(w) - (r + d(w))c}{r + d(w) + h(w)} - (r + \delta)k \right\}. \tag{3.37}$$

The first-order condition for an interior solution to the investment problem is

$$\frac{h(w)p'(k(w))}{r + d(w) + h(w)} = r + \delta. \tag{3.38}$$

The rate of return on capital, the left side of (3.38), is the product of the marginal product of capital $p'(k)$ and a factor reflecting the utilization of capital in the future. Since the job will be in one of two states in the future, vacant or filled, and the transition rate from a vacant to a filled job is equal to the acceptance probability, $h(\cdot)$, and the transition rate from filled to vacant is the separation probability, $d(\cdot)$, the ratio $h(\cdot)/[d(\cdot)+h(\cdot)]$ is the steady state fraction of time the job is filled or, equivalently, the capital utilization rate. The utilization factor is less than the utilization rate by the amount required to compensate for the fact that the job is vacant when created. Because the probability of acceptance is increasing in the rank of the wage offered, as represented by $F(w)$, while the separation rate is decreasing in the rank of the offer, the utilization factor increases with the wage offered. Because the second-order condition for an interior solution requires that $p(k)$ be strictly concave, the amount invested in general capital is increasing in the wage offer, that is, $k'(w) > 0$.

Because employers are all identical ex ante, optimality again requires that all wages offered yield the same profit in the sense that

$$\pi(w) = \arg\max_{k \geq 0} \left\{ \frac{[p(k)-w]h(w)-(r+d(w))c}{r+d(w)+h(w)} - (r+\delta)k \right\}$$

$$= \pi(b) \quad \forall w \in [b, \overline{w}]. \tag{3.39}$$

Finally, the equilibrium contact rate per worker, λ, satisfies the free entry condition

$$\pi(b) = \max_{k \geq 0} \left\{ \frac{[p(k)-w]\delta-(r+\delta)(\delta+\lambda)c}{(r+\delta)(\delta+\lambda)+\delta} - (r+\delta)k \right\} = 0, \tag{3.40}$$

where c represents the recruiting cost per worker contacted.

A steady state *labor market equilibrium*, then, is an aggregate contact rate per worker λ that satisfies (3.40), an offer distribution $F(w)$ that solves (3.39), and the optimal investment strategy $k(w)$ implicitly defined by (3.38). Because the right side of (3.40) is strictly decreasing in λ, it has a unique positive solution if and only if gross profit can exceed the cost of filling a vacant job in the sense that $p(k)-b > 0$ for some value of k. Since $\pi(w)$ is strictly decreasing in w while $h(w)$ is increasing and $d(w)$ is decreasing in F from equations (3.12) and (3.13), (3.39) has a unique solution for $F: [\underline{w}, \overline{w}] \to [0, 1]$. Finally, given the equilibrium values of λ and $F(w)$ just characterized, the associated investment function $k(w)$ is the unique solution to (3.38).

I compute a solution for the case of $b = 0$, a production function of the constant elasticity form $p(k) = k^\alpha$ with $\alpha = 0.85$, and the turnover parameters $\delta = 0.287$ and $\lambda = 0.207$ for the limiting case of $r = 0$.

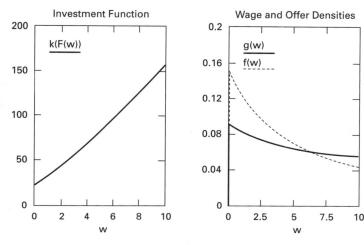

Figure 3.7
General capital investment.

The procedure is similar to that used in the match-specific capital case. First, the first-order condition for an optimal investment, equation (3.38), together with equations (3.12) and (3.13), are used to solve for $k(w)$ as a function of the offer c.d.f. $F(w)$. Given this solution, the unique value of c that solves (3.40) is found, and the value of $F(w)$ that satisfies (3.39) is computed for each w considered. Again, the associated steady state average wage paid distribution, $G(w)$ is computed using the steady state condition, equation (2.8). The results are illustrated in figure 3.7 where $f(w)$ and $g(w)$ are the derivatives of $F(w)$ and $G(w)$, respectively. The implied densities are again decreasing for similar parameter values.

3.5   Summary

As established in chapter 2, a single-period model of wage posting behavior can explain industry and size effects in wage equations if the productivity of the same worker varies across employers and the cost of recruiting workers is convex. In this chapter, I show that these same conditions are needed to explain the shape of the cross-firm distribution of average wages paid with a Burdett-Mortensen multiperiod extension of the original model. Specifically, the theory is consistent with the shapes of the wage and offer distributions found in Danish IDA data given a distribution of productivity with a long right tail.

The second principal result of the chapter is a demonstration that productive heterogeneity across firms can be the outcome of competition for workers by employers who are identical ex ante. Namely, employers who pay relatively more have an incentive to make a larger investment in capital specific to a match because the match separation rate is lower and in general capital because its utilization rate is higher. As cross-firm dispersion in wages is the only equilibrium outcome of the posting game played by identical employers, dispersion in productivity is a consequence, rather than a cause, of wage differences across employers in these versions of the model.

Notes

1. The IDA is a matched Danish employee-employer database constructed from data collected in an annual employment survey of all workplaces taken in November and from register data on individual workers. The data are organized as an annual panel of firms covering the period 1980–1995. The data set was created by Statistics Denmark and is maintained by the Centre for Labor and Social Research (CLS), located in Aarhus, Denmark. Online information about the data set can be found at <www.cls.dk>.

2. See Neal and Rosen (2000) for documentation of this fact.

3. I make this assumption throughout the chapter because it greatly simplifies the algebra without any material effect on the shape implications of the theory.

4

Wage Dispersion and Worker Flows

4.1 Introduction

Wage dispersion has allocative consequences. Workers have incentives to seek out and move to employers who offer higher pay and amenities. If differences in wage policies reflect market friction and differential productivity across firms, more productive employers recruit more workers as well as pay better. The resulting job-to-job mobility induced by search and recruiting efforts improves the allocation of labor resources. But competitive forces do not fully weed out inefficient employers. The empirical questions posed by this view of the labor market are many.

Do employed workers in fact move from lower- to higher-paying employers? If so, can one find evidence that workers invest search effort in the mobility process? Do differences in wage and recruiting policies reflect attempts by more productive employers to attract and retain workers? What is the distribution of productivity across employers that would support the wage dispersion observed in the data? How are wages set in labor markets characterized by imperfect job-to-job mobility? These are the questions raised in this chapter.

Bontemps, Robin, and van den Berg (1999, 2000) propose a semiparametric method of structural empirical inference that can be used to suggest answers to many of these questions in the context of models with search friction. The method is based on the fact that the structure of the wage policy in variants of the Burdett-Mortensen model with productive heterogeneity is identified by quantitative information implicit in the observed flow of workers from job to job, the size distribution of firms, and the cross-firm distribution of wages paid when the observations are interpreted as outcome of a labor market equilibrium. I consider two alternative wage determination hypotheses: an ex ante expected profit maximizing wage as proposed in the original Burdett and Mortensen (1998) paper and an ex post bilateral bargaining wage outcome in the tradition of the equilibrium matching models explored by Pissarides (2000).

The data used are cross-firm observations on wages paid by and worker flows into and out of Danish firms found in the IDA. For each privately owned firm in Denmark, observations of interest include the number of employees in November 1994, the number of these who were still employed the following November, the number of workers hired during the year and the prior employment status of each new hire, and the hourly wage earned by each employee during the year. From these observations, cross-firm distributions of average wages offered, average wages paid, and labor force size are constructed.

Using the IDA worker flows data, Christensen et al. (2001) estimate a model of job separation at the firm level that embeds investment in search effort as an endogenous choice made by each employed worker. Their results clearly support the hypothesis that workers invest in job-to-job mobility in response to the wage dispersion. In this chapter, I incorporate the Christensen et al. model of worker separation into the variants of the model studied here. Wage distribution information from the Danish IDA and the Christensen et al. estimates of the parameters of their separation model are then used to answer the questions posed earlier.

A principal finding is that the original Burdett-Mortensen monopsony model of wage determination with productive heterogeneity across firms is simply not consistent with the Danish IDA data in the sense that wages in the left tail of the observed average hourly wage distribution cannot be profit maximizing. In addition, monopsony profit is implausibly large on much of the portion of the support of the distribution for which observed wages are admissible.[1] However, a generalized Nash solution to the ex post bargaining problem faced by each worker-employer pair does imply a cross-firm relationship between the wage paid and labor productivity that is both consistent and plausible.

Given that the Nash bargaining outcome is a consistent explanation of differences in wages paid, the distribution of productivity that supports the wage and firm size distributions observed in the data can also be inferred. When workers obtain 50 percent or more of the surplus value of a match, the inferred distribution is unimodal but skewed with a very long right tail. Indeed, the symmetric Nash outcome implies that over half of the labor force employed by privately owned firms work for the most productive 1 percent. This inference seems to support the view that

the labor market allocates most workers to the relatively few employers who are significantly more productive than the typical firm, even
though search and recruiting friction permits considerable productive
heterogeneity across firms and wages are set to share these rents.

4.2   Structural Models of Wage Dispersion

4.2.1   Worker Search Strategy
In much of the existing literature applying the Burdett-Mortensen
approach to the analysis of labor market equilibrium, workers receive
offers at rates that are independent of their own effort. The only worker
decision of interest is to accept or not accept wage offers as they arrive.
Since the worker's incentive to seek a higher-paying job is increasing in
the difference between the worker's outside option and current wage,
this assumption is inappropriate. A model of endogenous search effort
choice is introduced in this section.

   In the worker flows data, there are two kinds of transitions: from
employment to unemployment and from one job to another. The employment hazard rate, denoted δ, is exogenous. Let s represent chosen
search effort, and assume that job offers arrive at rate λs where λ is a
search efficiency parameter. Each worker accepts an alternative if and
only if the expected present value of the future earning steam it offers is
higher. Given this specification, a worker's maximal value of a match-
paying wage w solves

$$rW(w) = \max_{s \geq 0} \left\{ \begin{array}{l} w + \delta\,[U - W(w)] \\ + \lambda s \int [\max \langle W(x),\, W(w)\rangle - W(w)]\,d\,F(x) - c_w(s) \end{array} \right\},$$

$$\text{(4.1)}$$

where U represents the value of unemployment, $c_w(s)$ denotes the cost
of search effort, and r is the risk-free interest rate. Equation (4.1) is a
continuous-time Bellman equation that reflects the optimal search effort
choice problem as well as the exogenous outcomes that occur in the case
of job destruction and job-to-job movement for other reasons. Similarly,
the value of unemployment solves

$$rU = \max_{s_0 \geq 0} \left\{ b + \lambda s_0 \int [\max \langle W(w),\, U\rangle - U]\,d\,F(w) - c_w(s_0) \right\}, \qquad \text{(4.2)}$$

where b represents income flow received when unemployed. Since $W(w)$
is an increasing function, the worker accepts employment only if the

wage offered exceeds the reservation wage, R, defined by

$$U = W(R). \tag{4.3}$$

Because the derivative of the value of employment function is

$$W'(w) = \frac{1}{r + \delta + \lambda s(w)[1 - F(w)]} > 0 \tag{4.4}$$

by the envelope theorem, an employed worker quits to take an alternative job offer if and only if it pays a higher wage. Hence, optimal search effort maximizes the difference between the total return and cost of search in the sense that

$$s(w) = \arg\max_{s \geq 0} \left\{ \lambda s \int_w^{\overline{w}} [W(x) - W(w)] \, dF(x) - c_w(s) \right\}$$

$$= \arg\max_{s \geq 0} \left\{ \lambda s \int_w^{\overline{w}} W'(x)[1 - F(x)] \, dx - c_w(s) \right\}$$

$$= \arg\max_{s \geq 0} \left\{ \lambda s \int_w^{\overline{w}} \left(\frac{1 - F(x)}{r + \delta + \lambda s(x)[1 - F(x)]} \right) dx - c_w(s) \right\}, \tag{4.5}$$

where integration by parts yields the second equality and equation (4.4) implies the third. Given $c_w(s)$ strictly convex, the optimal search effort strategy $s(w)$ is monotone decreasing in w. Furthermore, because the first-order condition,

$$c_w'(s(w)) = \lambda \int_w^{\overline{w}} [W(x) - W(w)] \, dF(x), \tag{4.6}$$

characterizes the optimal solution when $c_w(0) = c_w'(0) = 0$, the net value of employment can be written as

$$W(w) - U$$
$$= \frac{w - b + [s(w)c_w'(s(w)) - c_w(s(w))] - [s(R)c_w'(s(R)) - c_w(s(R))]}{r + \delta} \tag{4.7}$$

from equations (4.1) and (4.2) where R is the reservation wage defined by equation (4.3).

Because acceptance of an offer when unemployed requires that $w \geq R$, equations (4.1), (4.2), and (4.3) together imply that the search intensity of an unemployed worker is the same as that of a worker employed at the reservation wage provided that the reservation wage is the unemployment benefit,

$$s_0 = s(R), \tag{4.8}$$

and the reservation wage is equal to the unemployment benefit,

$$R = b. \tag{4.9}$$

The last result, the implied exogeneity of the reservation wage, requires that both the search cost function $c_w(s)$ and the search efficiency parameter λ be independent of employment status. In the existing empirical search literature, offer arrival rates are typically regarded as exogenous. In this case, (4.9) holds if and only if the offer arrival rates are the same when employed as they are when unemployed. This necessary and sufficient condition for an exogenous reservation wage violates the empirical inference drawn from the data that worker receive offers less frequently when employed. However, in the endogenous search effort model, workers have less incentive to search when employed than when unemployed. Hence, an exogenous reservation wage and a lower offer arrival rate for employed workers are mutually consistent in the extended model.

4.2.2 Steady-State Relationships

According to the model, δ represents the rate of worker transition from employment to unemployment, and $\lambda s(b)$ is a worker's transition rate from unemployment to employment. Hence, steady-state unemployment rate solves

$$\frac{u}{1 - u} = \frac{\delta}{\lambda s(b)} \tag{4.10}$$

given that the aggregate labor force is represented by the unit interval.

The gross flow of workers into jobs that pay w or less is composed of unemployed workers who become employed in a job of the category. The outflow is equal to the sum of the jobs lost through destruction plus the flow of employed workers who seek and find a higher-paying job. Equating the net inflow and outflow yields the steady-state relationship between the fraction of offers no greater than w, $F(w)$, and the fraction of workers employed by firms paying wage w or less, denoted $G(w)$, that is,

$$\delta G(w) + \lambda[1 - F(w)] \int_{\underline{w}}^{w} s(x) \, dG(x) = \frac{u \lambda F(w)}{1 - u} = \delta F(w), \tag{4.11}$$

where the second equality follows from (4.10). Given the functions $s(w)$ and $F(w)$ and the parameters δ and λ, a unique solution to the integral equation (4.11) can be shown to exist for $G(w)$.

4.2.3 Employer Recruiting Policy

The probability that a random applicant accepts the wage offer w, denoted $h(w)$, is the fraction of the applicant flow willing to accept the wage w. Because those willing to accept include the unemployed and the employed seeking a higher wage, and because the latter flow given current employment at wage $z < w$ is $s(z)G'(z)(1 - u)$,

$$h(w) = \frac{\lambda s(b)u + \lambda \int_{\underline{w}}^{w} s(z)\, dG(z)(1 - u)}{\lambda s(b)u + \lambda \int_{\underline{w}}^{\overline{w}} s(z)\, dG(z)(1 - u)} = \frac{\delta + \lambda \int_{\underline{w}}^{w} s(z)\, dG(z)}{\delta + \lambda \int_{\underline{w}}^{\overline{w}} s(z)\, dG(z)}, \qquad (4.12)$$

where the second equality is obtained by using (4.10) to eliminate u. The same firm's separation rate is the sum of the exogenous turnover rate plus the rate at which employees find a higher-paying job,

$$d(w) = \delta + \lambda s(w)[1 - F(w)]. \qquad (4.13)$$

The firm's value of employing a worker solves the Bellman equation $rJ(p, w) = p - w - d(w)J(p, w)$, which implies

$$J(p, w) = \frac{p - w}{r + d(w)}. \qquad (4.14)$$

As mentioned earlier, the expected profit per worker contacted is

$$\pi(p, w) = h(w)J(p, w) = \frac{h(w)(p - w)}{r + d(w)}. \qquad (4.15)$$

Given the wage paid, the optimal recruiting effort maximizes the difference between expected present value attributable to recruiting activity net of recruiting cost. Denote the contact frequency as ηv and let $c_f(v)$ represent recruiting cost where v is a measure of recruiting effort, call it "vacancies," and η is the efficiency of recruiting effort. Formally, optimal recruiting effort is defined by

$$v(p, w) = \arg\max_{v \geq 0}\{\eta v \pi(p, w) - c_f(v)\}. \qquad (4.16)$$

Under the assumption that the cost of recruiting function is strictly convex and satisfies the boundary conditions $c_f(0) = c'_f(0) = 0$, then the optimal choice satisfies the first-order condition for an interior solution

$$c'_f(v(p, w)) = \eta\pi(p, w) \tag{4.17}$$

if and only if $\eta\pi(p, w) \geq 0$. Given the wage paid, the optimal contact frequency is increasing in employer productivity because $\pi(p, w)$ is increasing in p given w.

4.2.4 Wage Determination

A Burdett-Mortensen monopsonist chooses an ex ante wage policy to maximize profit per worker contacted, that is,

$$w_1(p) = \arg\max_{w \geq b} \pi(p, w) = \arg\max_{w \geq b} \left\{ \frac{h(w)(p - w)}{r + d(w)} \right\}. \tag{4.18}$$

Alternatively, if the wage is set ex post as the outcome of a generalized Nash bilateral bargaining problem, a plausible specification of the outcome is

$$w_2(p) = \arg\max_{w \geq b} (W(w) - U)^\beta J(p, w)^{1-\beta}$$

$$= \arg\max_{w \geq b} (W(w) - U)^\beta \left(\frac{p - w}{r + d(w)} \right)^{1-\beta} \tag{4.19}$$

where $\beta \in (0, 1)$ is a parameter reflecting the worker's "bargaining power."[2] Given either wage determination mechanism, the wage outcome is increasing in employer productivity.[3]

In what follows, p is assumed to be continuously distributed over the interval $[\underline{p}, \bar{p}]$ representing the set of participating firms. Under this assumption, both $w_1(p)$ and $w_2(p)$ are strictly increasing in p. The upper support $\bar{p}$ is given but the lower support $\underline{p}$ must be large enough to induce participation by all firms with greater productivity. Since any firm willing to recruit is a participant and the least productive participants pay the lowest wage, the necessary and sufficient condition for participation is

$$v(p, w(p)) > 0 \Leftrightarrow \pi(p, w(p)) > 0 \Leftrightarrow p > w(p) \quad \text{for all } p > \underline{p}$$

under either wage determination hypothesis given a strictly convex recruiting cost function with the property $c_f(0) = c'_f(0) = 0$. In other words, a firm participates if and only if its productivity exceeds the wage paid. As an implication $\underline{p} = \underline{w}$ characterizes the marginal participant. This fact together with (4.18) and (4.19) require

$$\underline{p} = w(\underline{p}) = \underline{w} = R = b, \tag{4.20}$$

under either wage determination hypothesis, that is, the marginal participant pays the reservation wage and makes no profit. Specifically, if $\underline{p} = w(\underline{p}) > b$, the least productive firm can make a positive profit by paying the reservation wage in the monopsony case and, if $\underline{p} > b$, then $\underline{p} > w(\underline{p}) > b$ in the bilateral bargaining case. Of course, $\overline{p} > b$ is an obvious necessary as well as sufficient requirement for trade.

4.2.5 Aggregation

Because any worker meets a specific employer at rates that are proportional to the recruiting effort of the latter and because the relationship between wage and employer productivity is monotone increasing under either wage determination mechanism, the offer distribution is the "vacancy" weighted distribution of wages

$$F(w(p)) = \frac{\int_{\underline{p}}^{p} v(z, w(z))\, d\Gamma(z)}{\int_{\underline{p}}^{\overline{p}} v(z, w(z))\, d\Gamma(z)}, \tag{4.21}$$

where $\Gamma(p)$ represents the fraction of employers with productivity p or less. In other words, the offer distribution is the fraction of vacancies offered by firms who pay $w(p)$ or less.

The search and recruiting efficiency parameters, λ and η, generally depend on the search and recruiting effort of other workers and employers participating in the market. In the matching theory branch of the search equilibrium literature, this relationship is characterized by an aggregate "matching function." (See Pissarides 2000 for an extensive discussion of the concept and its applications.) Here I assume that the total flow of matches is proportional to the product of aggregate recruiting effort and aggregate search effort. More precisely, as each worker contacts employers at rate $\lambda s(x)$ where $x = b$ if unemployed and $x = w$ if employed at wage w, the aggregate flow of contacts per period is given by

$$M = \lambda \left(us(b) + (1 - u) \int_{\underline{w}}^{\overline{w}} s(w)\, dG(w) \right).$$

Analogously, the flow of meetings must also satisfy

$$M = \eta m \int_{\underline{p}}^{\overline{p}} v(z, w(z)) \, d\Gamma(z),$$

where m is the number of employers per worker because each employer of type p paying a wage equal to $w(p)$ contacts workers at rate $\eta v(p, w(p))$. It follows that $M = \lambda \eta$, where

$$\lambda = m \int_{\underline{p}}^{\overline{p}} v(z, w(z)) \, d\Gamma(z)$$

$$\eta = us(b) + (1 - u) \int s(w) \, dG(w),$$

(4.22)

is a consistent specification of the matching technology. Note that if only unemployed workers were to search and all employers were identical, this specification would reduce to a matching function of the form $M = ms(b)vu$. More general specifications of the matching function exist that also satisfy the necessary aggregation conditions; the existence proof that follows is restricted to what some refer to as the "quadratic" case for simplicity. Although special, it adequately accounts for the complementarity of search and recruiting effort in the matching process emphasized in the literature. (See Mortensen and Pissarides (1999a,b) for more on this point.)

4.2.6   Labor Market Equilibrium

I am finally prepared to define the market solution concept for the extended model:

Definition.   A *steady state labor market equilibrium* is composed of functions $s : [\underline{w}, \overline{w}] \to \mathbb{R}_+$, $v : [\underline{p}, \overline{p}] \times [\underline{w}, \overline{w}] \to \mathbb{R}_+$, $w : [\underline{p}, \overline{p}] \to [\underline{w}, \overline{w}]$ that are respectively optimal in the sense that the search strategy $s(w)$ solves (4.5), the recruiting strategy $v(p, w)$ solves (4.16), and the wage policy $w(p)$ is either the solution to (4.18) or to (4.19) together with the value of employment function $W : [\underline{w}, \overline{w}] \to \mathbb{R}_+$ defined by (4.1), value of employment U defined by (4.2), wage offer c.d.f. $F : [\underline{w}, \overline{w}] \to [0, 1]$ defined by (4.21), matching efficiency parameters λ and η defined by (4.22), and steady state unemployment rate u and wage c.d.f. $G : [\underline{w}, \overline{w}] \to [0, 1]$ that solve (4.10) and (4.11), respectively. The equilibrium is monopsonistic if $w(p)$ satisfies (4.18) and is a bilateral bargaining equilibrium if $w(p)$ satisfies (4.19).

The following assumptions, all of which have previously been introduced informally, are maintained:

Assumption 1. The interest rate r, employment hazard δ, number of firms per worker m, and unemployment benefit b are all positive constants.

Assumption 2. The set of firms is represented by a continuous and differentiable distribution of productivity $\Gamma : [0, \bar{p}] \to [0, 1]$. The exogenous upper support is finite and exceeds the unemployment benefit, namely, $\infty > \bar{p} > b$.

Assumption 3. The cost of search, $c_w(s)$, is increasing, strictly convex, and twice differentiable, and it has the property $c_w(0) = c'_w(0) = 0$.

Assumption 4. The cost of recruiting, $c_f(v)$, is increasing, strictly convex, and twice differentiable, and it has the property $c_f(0) = c'_f(0) = 0$.

In chapter 3, existence for special cases was established by showing that an equilibrium is isomorphic to a particular solution to some well-behaved system of ordinary differential equations. A similar approach applies in this more general case as well.

Proposition 3. A unique steady state labor market equilibrium exists with the property that $(\lambda, \eta) > 0$ in both the monopsony and bilateral bargaining cases.

Proof. See the mathematical appendix.

Although it is of no particular interest, it can be shown that a no-trade equilibrium, one with the property $\lambda = \eta = 0$, always exists as well. However, the fact that one and only one equilibrium exists in which trade takes place is of note.

4.3 Empirical Inference

4.3.1 Job Separation Flows in the IDA
Christensen et al. (2001) use observations on worker separations at the firm level in the IDA to estimate the turnover parameters given a cost of search effort function of the power form

$$c_w(s) = \frac{c_0 s^{1+\frac{1}{\alpha}}}{1 + \frac{1}{\alpha}}. \tag{4.23}$$

The first-order condition for an optimal search effort choice, equation (4.6), can be written as

$$s(w) = \left(\frac{1}{c_0} \int_w^{\bar{w}} \frac{\lambda[1 - F(x)]\,dx}{r + \delta + \lambda s(x)[1 - F(x)]} \right)^{\alpha} \tag{4.24}$$

in this case. Estimates of the cost and turnover parameters, δ, λ, c_0, and α, are obtained by finding those values that maximize the likelihood of the observed number of separations experienced by all the firms in the IDA during the year beginning in November 1994. Since the duration of a job spell with a firm paying wage w is exponential with parameter equal to the separation rate,

$$d(w) = \delta + \lambda s(w)[1 - F(w)], \tag{4.25}$$

the number of workers who stay with the firm is binomially distributed with "sample size" equal to firm size n and "probability of success" equal to $e^{-d(w)}$. Under the assumption that the parameters are identical across firms, the maximum likelihood estimates conditional on the interest rate r and offer distribution F are

$$(c_0, \delta, \lambda, \alpha) = \arg\max \sum_i [(n_i - x_i) \ln(1 - e^{-d(w_i)}) - d(w_i)x_i],$$

where w_i represents the wage paid by firm i, n_i the firm's size, and x_i the number of stayers, those who were employed throughout the year. Given that a choice of units is arbitrary, search effort at the reservation wage, $s(b)$, can be normalized to unity without loss of generality. Given the offer c.d.f. $F(w)$ observed in the data, an annual interest rate r equal to 0.045 per annum, and the normalization $s(b) = 1$, the estimates of the parameters of interest are $\delta = 0.287$ and $\lambda = 0.593$ per annum and $\alpha = 1.105$.[4] (Because the sample size is very large, the precision of the estimates is virtually certain to the third significant digit.)

Given the cost function specified in equation (4.23), the fact that the estimate of the elasticity of search effort with respect to the return to search, α, is close to unity suggests that the cost of search function is reasonably approximated by a quadratic. The arrival rate parameter estimates reflect relatively high turnover in the Danish labor market. Indeed, the value of the sum $\delta + \lambda s(b) = 0.287 + 0.593 = 0.88$ implies that the expected job duration of a worker employed at the lowest-paying firm is only 1.14 years.

Indeed, the Christensen et al. (2001) value of the intercept of the separation function, δ, is much too large to be interpreted as the transition
rate to unemployment. For example, Rosholm and Svarer (2000) estimate the employment spell hazard is only 0.099 per annum using panel
data on Danish worker labor market event histories for the 1980s.[5] Since
the worker destination was not used in estimating δ, the difference,
$\delta_1 = \delta - \delta_0 = 0.287 - 0.099 = 0.188$, might be interpreted as turnover that
is not explicitly motivated by wage differences. Furthermore, if an unemployed worker searches for an acceptable job at rate $\delta_1 + \lambda s(b)$ while the
same worker when employed at wage w transits to another job drawn
at random at rate δ_1 and to a higher paying job at rate $\lambda s(w)[1 - F(w)]$,
then the steady state conditions (4.10) is replaced by

$$\frac{u}{1-u} = \frac{\delta_0}{\delta_1 + \lambda s(b)}.$$

Although the flow of workers into the set employed at wage w or less
now includes those who move across jobs for nonwage reasons, the
steady-state condition

$$\delta G(w) + \lambda[1 - F(w)] \int_{\underline{w}}^{w} s(x)\,dG(x)$$

$$= \frac{[u(\delta_1 + \lambda s(b)) + (1 - u)\delta_1]\,F(w)}{1-u} = \delta F(w)$$

is the same as (4.11). Using the Rosholm and Svarer estimate of $\delta_0 =
0.099$, the implied steady state value of the unemployment rate is $u =
\delta_0/(\delta + \lambda) = 0.099/0.88 = 0.1125$, which compares favorably with the
12.2 percent unemployment rate actually recorded for Denmark in 1994.
Indeed, all the other derivations mentioned earlier continue to hold as
well given this reinterpretation of the intercept parameter δ.

4.3.2   Danish Wage Setting Institutions

Any attempt to use the tools of labor market analysis developed in this
paper to explain cross-firm dispersion in Danish wages raises questions
about the institutional context of wage determination in the Danish private sector. As is well known, Danish unionization rates are among
the highest in the industrialized world. Indeed, a virtual constellation
of organizations composed of trade unions on the one side and employer's organizations on the other engage in a synchronized collective
bargaining round every two years. Their agreements determine a set

of labor contracts covering almost all privately employed participants in the Danish labor market. In addition to wages and work rules, the collective agreements, rather than formal government legislation, specify general conditions of the employment relationship for the nation as a whole. For example, there is no government-mandated minimum wage above and beyond those specified by collective agreement, and there is no legislated employment protection policy. Even unemployment compensation is a voluntary system administered through unions rather than a government agency.

In their recent history and analysis of what they dub the "Danish Model" of collective bargaining, Due et al. (1994, 12) argue that the system, born in the dawn of the last century, is more than a market mechanism for the determination of wages.[6] In their words, "The emergence of Denmark's welfare state can be attributed to the capacity of the Danish system of organizations and collective bargaining—and a comprehensively organized labor market—to serve as an arena for resolving conflicts of interest in society, thereby making a vital contribution towards stable economic and political development." That said, the Danish bargaining process has experienced considerable structural change as a wage determination mechanism in the last two decades of the twentieth century. Indeed, the recent evolution of the system is the principal subject of their book.

The main changes in the bargaining process documented by Due et al. can be summarized as follows. First, the sheer number of different agreements have been reduced from a collection of over six hundred, each covering a different trade or occupation, to between ten and twenty comprehensive framework agreements. Second, the agreements made in recent bargaining rounds tend to specify minimum pay and working conditions across a broad spectrum of trades and industries rather than dictate actual wages paid. The details of both wages and work rules are worked out, subject to the minimums specified in the applicable framework agreement, at the firm level. As a quantitative measure of the evolution in this direction, the authors note that so-called flexible pay systems that allow for local determination of wages and working conditions were already embedded in 65 percent of all central agreements by 1989. The fraction grew to 80 percent in the 1991 round of agreements and to 85 percent in 1993. Although the reasons for these changes are many, the fact that wages in the private sector were largely determined at the firm level in the year starting November 1994, used here, suggests that decentralized models of wage determination are potentially useful for explaining cross-firm wage dispersion in Denmark.

4.3.3   Monopsony Wage

Recall that the optimal monopsony wage is defined by

$$w(p) = \arg\max_{w \geq b} \pi(p, w). \tag{4.26}$$

Following Bontemps, Robin, and van den Berg (2000), the observed wage distribution is *admissible* under the monopsony hypothesis if and only if every element of its support could be profit maximizing for some level of (unobserved) productivity. Equivalently, the relationship between the wage and firm productivity implied by the observed wage distribution and the worker turnover behavior must be monotone increasing. This relationship can be derived using the following first-order condition for the monopsony wage:

$$\frac{h'(w)}{h(w)} - \frac{d'(w)}{r + d(w)} - \frac{1}{p - w} = 0. \tag{4.27}$$

Specifically, since the Christensen et al. (2001) results and the observed wage distribution provide empirical estimates of the acceptance and separation functions, $h(w)$ and $d(w)$, the implied inverse of the wage policy function,

$$p(w) = w \left[1 + \frac{1}{\frac{wh'(w)}{h(w)} - \frac{wd'(w)}{r + d(w)}} \right], \tag{4.28}$$

can be computed for all wage rates in the support of the distribution.

To compute $h(w)$ and $d(w)$, I use the Christensen et al. (2001) estimates of the parameters of the separation function and the search effort function reported earlier, a smooth approximation to the distribution of average wages paid illustrated in figure 4.1, and the associated offer distribution implied by the steady-state conditions. In other words, the parameter estimates and $G(w)$ are used to compute $h(w)$ as specified in equation (4.12), and $d(w)$ is then computed using equation (4.13) where

$$F(w) = \frac{\delta G(w) + \lambda \int_{\underline{w}}^{w} s(x)\,dG(x)}{\delta + \lambda \int_{\underline{w}}^{\overline{w}} s(x)\,dG(x)}$$

from the steady-state condition (4.11). The associated wage and offer probability density functions are illustrated in figure 4.1. The implied acceptance probability and separation rate functions are plotted in figure 4.2.

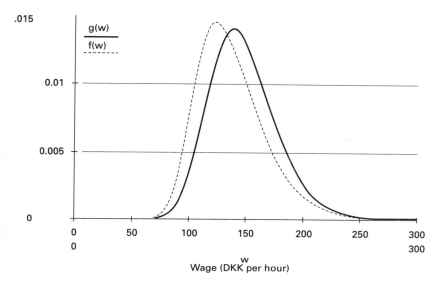

Figure 4.1
Smoothed wage $g(w)$ and offer $f(w)$ probability density functions.

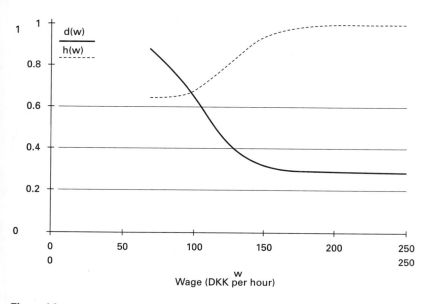

Figure 4.2
The separation $d(w)$ and acceptance probability $h(w)$ functions.

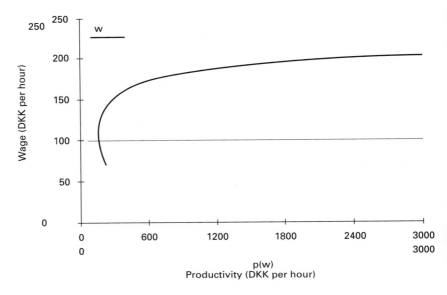

Figure 4.3
Inferred monopsony wage policy function.

The wage policy function $w(p)$ implied by equation (4.28) is illustrated in figure 4.3. The curve is a plot of w against $p(w)$ for a set of values that cover the support of the observed wage distribution. Because the curve is negatively sloped for wage rates below 105 DKK per hour, each associated wage rate in this region minimizes, rather than maximizes, profit. In other words, there is no level of productivity for any one of the wages observed that maximizes profit. Approximately, 13 percent of all offers made are in the inadmissible region and 6 percent of employed workers earn such a wage. These facts imply that the observed wage distribution cannot be an equilibrium outcome of the model.

Over the remaining admissible range, the wage increases rapidly with productivity initially but then the rate of increase falls dramatically. As a consequence, the implied ratios of productivity to wage are implausibly large over much of the wage support. For example, at the median wage earned, equal to 144 DKK per hour, "monopsony power" as reflected in the ratio of rent to the wage, $(p(w) - w)/w$ is equal to 60 percent. At the ninetieth percentile, $w = 186$ DKK per hour, the implied value of p is 2, 720 DKK per hour, which implies that marginal productivity is almost 6.5 times the wage while at the 95th percentile, $w = 200$ DKK per hour, the ratio is equal to 12. These inferences are hardly plausible even if the wage distribution were otherwise admissible.

The reason inferred monopsony rents are large and increase so dramatically with productivity is reflected in the first-order condition for an optimal wage choice, as expressed in equation (4.28), and the shapes of the acceptance probability, $h(w)$, and separation rate, $d(w)$, illustrated in figure 4.2. The first-order condition for an optimal choice implies that the monopsony rent measured at any level of productivity is approximately equal to the inverse of the sum of the elasticities of the separation rate function and the acceptance probability function. Both functions are relatively elastic at low wages but converge to constants as the wage tends to the upper support. In other words, a small wage differential in the lower range of the support has a substantial impact on an employer's ability to both attract and retain workers, but the same differential in the upper reaches has little or no effect on either. Clearly, the reason for the differences in the response of the separation rate function at different wage levels is that the relatively well paid workers have less incentive to invest in search than do low-paid workers and workers employed by firms paying wages near the upper support have no incentive at all. For the same reason, an employer is more likely to contact a lower- than a higher-paid worker given that contact frequencies across workers reflect relative search intensities.

4.3.4 Bilateral Bargaining

Perhaps it is not surprising that Danish data reject the monopsony hypothesis given the long history of collective bargaining in Denmark. Still, the work of Christensen et al. (2001) clearly documents both the existence of large cross-firm wage differentials and worker movement away from low-paying firms. A system of agreements based on bilateral bargaining at the firm level represents a decentralized wage setting mechanism in which workers capture some share of the quasi rents associated with the existence of a match. In this section, I ask whether the Nash bilateral bargaining model is consistent with the Danish data on the distribution of average wages paid.

After they meet, the net value to a worker of employment at a job paying wage w is the difference between the expected future income when employed and not employed, the surplus value $W(w) - U$. To an employer with labor productivity p, the value of the firm of employing any worker at wage w is the expected present value of future profit denoted $J(p, w)$. The generalized Nash equilibrium wage outcome is defined by

$$w(p) = \arg\max_{w \geq b}\{[W(w) - U]^{\beta} J(p, w)^{1-\beta}\}, \tag{4.29}$$

where $\beta \in (0, 1)$ represents the worker "bargaining power" parameter and

$$J(p, w) = \frac{p - w}{r + d(w)}$$

denotes the employer's value of hiring a worker.

The first-order condition for an interior optimal wage choice as specified in equation (4.29) can be written as

$$\beta \left(\frac{W'(w)}{W(w) - U}\right) - (1 - \beta)\left(\frac{d'(w)}{r + d(w)} + \frac{1}{p - w}\right) = 0. \tag{4.30}$$

Compared with the first-order condition for the case of monopsony as expressed in equation (4.27), an expression proportional to the elasticity of the worker's surplus value of employment replaces the elasticity of the acceptance probability in this expression. Indeed, the inverse of the implied wage policy function is

$$p(w) = w\left[1 + \frac{1}{\left(\frac{\beta}{1-\beta}\right)\frac{wW'(w)}{W(w) - U} - \frac{wd'(w)}{r + d(w)}}\right]. \tag{4.31}$$

Again, admissibility of the hypothesis that wages are determined as the outcome of a bilateral bargain requires that the function $p(w)$ implied by the data is monotone increasing.

To compute the inferred inverse policy function, $p(w)$, one needs the empirical counterparts of surplus value, $W(w) - U$, as well as the separation rate function, $d(w)$, for all wages in the support of the wage distribution. Given the cost function specification assumed and the parameters estimated by Christensen et al. (2001), the net value of employment can be computed using equation (4.7). The resulting surplus value of employment function, defined as $S(w) = W(w) - U$, is illustrated in figure 4.4. As it should be, the function is increasing and convex in the wage earned and zero at the reservation wage $b = \underline{w}$.

The empirical wage policy function, $w(p)$, for a symmetric bilateral bargaining wage outcome, that associated with the case of equal bargaining power $\beta = 0.5$, is illustrated in figure 4.5 as the solid curve. The

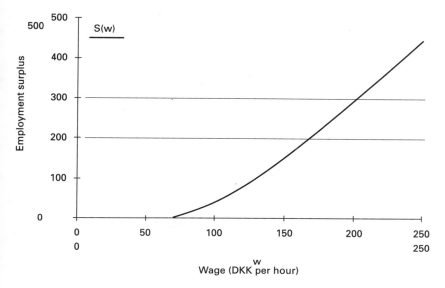

Figure 4.4
Surplus value of employment function: $S(w) = W(w) - U$.

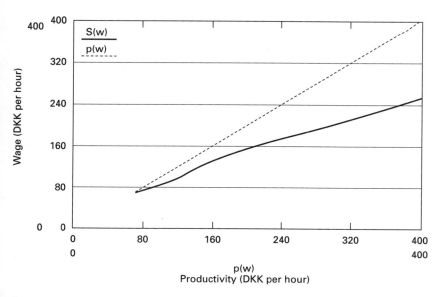

Figure 4.5
Inferred bilateral bargaining wage function.

45 degree ray is included for reference as the dotted line. Obviously, the function is very different from that illustrated in figure 4.3 for the hypothetical monopsony wage case. First, it is admissible for all observed wage rates, that is, a level of firm productivity exists such that every observed wage is a solution to the symmetric Nash bilateral bargaining problem for some choice-appropriate value of p. Second, a computation exercise verifies that this conclusion is true for almost all strictly positive values β in the unit interval.[7]

A comparison of equations (4.28) and (4.31) together with an observation of the shape of the surplus value of employment function illustrated in figure 4.4 reveals the reason for a monotonic relationship between wage and productivity. Namely, because $W(w) - U$ is quite elastic throughout its range, the implied wage increases with p at a rate that reflects the magnitude of the worker's bargaining power parameter β. Indeed, because workers do not search on the job and, consequently, $d'(w) = 0$, $w'(p) = \beta$ is a standard result in the matching literature. (See Pissarides (2000).) Since $d(w)$ is flat for all wages above the median of the distribution of wages paid, $w \geq 144$ DKK in the case at hand, $w'(p) = \beta$ holds as an approximation on that interval. The slope is larger than β in the range for which the separation function is elastic because bargaining pairs have an incentive to set the wage policy in part to discourage worker search in the future if a surplus exists in the sense that match productivity exceeds the reservation wage.

4.3.5   Firm Productivity
The distribution of productivity required to support the observed distribution of wages paid when the wage for each match is a symmetric bilateral bargaining outcome ($\beta = 0.5$) is derived in this section. Because the rate of increase in the wage paid with respect to firm productivity is less than unity, expected profit per worker contacted, $\pi(p, w(p))$, is increasing in p from (4.15). Hence, recruiting effort as a function of firm productivity, $v(p, w(p))$, is increasing in p from (4.16), which in turn implies that the mean of the ergodic distribution of firm size,

$$n(p) = \frac{v(p, w(p))h(w(p))}{d(w(p))}, \qquad (4.32)$$

is also monotone increasing in p. This fact allows one to identify the distribution of productivity that underlies the wage distribution from the observed distributions of wage paid and firm size.

Because $w(p)$ is strictly increasing, the wage c.d.f. can be written as

$$G(w(p)) = \frac{\int_{\underline{p}}^{p} n(x)\, d\Gamma(x)}{\int_{\underline{p}}^{\bar{p}} n(x)\, d\Gamma(x)}. \tag{4.33}$$

The fact that $n(p)$ is also monotone increasing in p implies

$$Q(n(p)) = \frac{\int_{\underline{p}}^{p} d\Gamma(x)}{\int_{\underline{p}}^{\bar{p}} d\Gamma(x)}, \tag{4.34}$$

where $Q(n)$ denotes the firm size cumulative distribution function. By using the differential forms of equations (4.33) and (4.34),

$$G'(w(p))w'(p) = n(p)\Gamma'(p)$$

and

$$Q'(n(p))n'(p) = \Gamma'(p) \tag{4.35}$$

to eliminate $\Gamma'(p)$, one obtains

$$G'(w(p))w'(p)En = n(p)Q'(n(p))n'(p), \tag{4.36}$$

where

$$En = \frac{\int_{\underline{p}}^{\bar{p}} n(x)\, d\Gamma(x)}{\int_{\underline{p}}^{\bar{p}} d\Gamma(x)} = \int_{\underline{n}}^{\bar{n}} n\, dQ(n) \tag{4.37}$$

is the average size of a firm in the population.
Let

$$N(w) = n(p(w)) \tag{4.38}$$

represent the size of a firm that pays wage w. Then, equation (4.36) can be written as a first-order differential equation

$$N'(w) = \frac{g(w)En}{q(w)N(w)}. \tag{4.39}$$

Given the empirical counterparts of $g(w) = G'(w)$, $q(w) = Q'(w)$, and En, this equation can be solved to find the particular solution satisfying the boundary condition implicitly defined by (4.37). The distribution of productivity across firms that supports the observed wage distribution

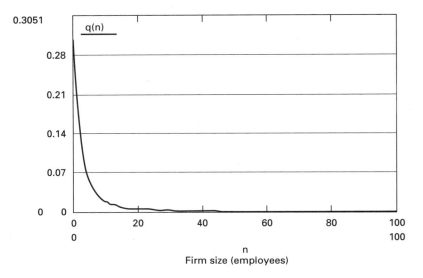

Figure 4.6
IDA firm size probability density function, $q\,(n)$.

can be recovered with knowledge of $p'(w)$ and $N(w)$. Namely, from equation (4.35), (4.39), and (4.37), the cross-firm productivity density function is

$$\Gamma'(p(w)) = \frac{q\,(N(w))N'(w)}{p'(w)} = \frac{g(w)En}{p'(w)N(w)}. \tag{4.40}$$

A continuous approximation to the firm size density actually observed in the IDA is illustrated in figure 4.6. Note that almost all firms are quite small. Indeed, 26.5 percent employ a single wage earner and 62 percent have four or fewer. Only 9 percent of the firms are composed of more than twenty employees, and only 3 percent have more than fifty workers. Still, there are a few immense firms. The obvious skew in the distribution is reflected in the fact that the median size lies between two and three employees while the average is 13.2.

Finally, the curve of the productivity probability density function implied by the firm size density, the expected size function, and the wage policy function as expressed in equation (4.40) is plotted in figure 4.7. The resulting probability density is unimodal but with a rather long right tail. The firms with productivity less than the mode, which happens to be $p = 135$ DKK per hour approximately, employ only 11 percent of all

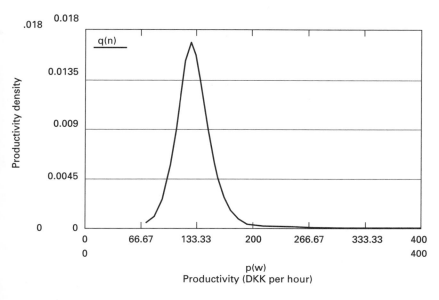

Figure 4.7
Inferred productivity p.d.f., $\phi(p)$.

workers in the private sector. The productivity of the firm paying the median wage, 144 DKK per hour, is 179 DKK per hour. Obviously, this firm is in the far right tail of the distribution of productivity. Indeed, given that the inferred labor force size is 201 workers at the median wage, the observed size distribution implies that less than 1 percent of all firms are larger. Hence, the data and model imply that over half of all Danish workers in the private sector are employed by the largest and most productive 1 percent of the firms.

4.3.6   The Cost of Hiring

In principle, one can also derive an estimate of the cost of hiring the marginal worker from the information at hand. Namely, the first-order condition for an optimal recruiting effort choice, equation (4.17), can be written as

$$MCH(w) = \frac{c'_f(v(p(w), w))}{\eta h(w)} = \frac{p(w) - w}{r + d(w)}. \qquad (4.41)$$

The left side is the marginal cost of recruiting effort per period multiplied by the expected time required to fill a vacancy, and the right side is the expected present value of future profit attributable to hiring the worker where $p(w)$ is the inverse of the wage policy function. Given that the hire flow equals the separation flow on average in steady state, an estimate of the marginal cost of hiring can be computed by plotting $MCH(w)$ against

$$H(w) = d(w)N(w), \tag{4.42}$$

where $N(w)$ is the size-wage relations that solves (4.39). An upward sloping relationship is, of course, necessary for optimality.

The relationship inferred from the observed wage and size distribution data and the separations model is illustrated as figure 4.8 given equal shares of match rents, namely, $\beta = 0.5$. The curve implies that marginal recruiting costs do increase with the hire flow. Indeed, the shape of the curve suggests the existence of an effective capacity constraint on any firm's hire flow equal to about ninety workers per year. As the implied hire flow for the firm offering the wage at the 90th percentile of the wage distribution is eighty-five workers per year, this constraint limits the growth of the very few most productive employers.

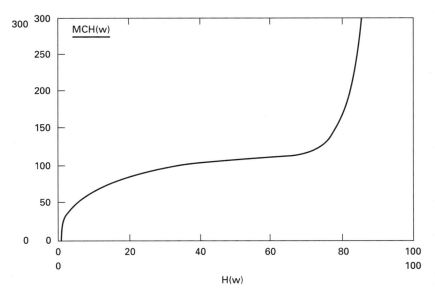

Figure 4.8
Marginal cost of hiring curve.

For firms offering the median wage of 144 DKK per hour, the hire flow is thirty workers per year and the marginal cost of hiring the marginal worker is quite high, about 67 percent of the annual wage. The average hiring cost is lower, about 52 percent of the annual wage. Although the shape of the marginal cost curve is not, the cost estimates are very sensitive to the unknown worker's assumed share parameter. Indeed, for $\beta = 0.75$ instead of 0.5 the implied costs are roughly half as large. Numbers of this magnitude are quite consistent with the recruiting and hiring cost surveys reported by Hamermesh (1993).

4.4 Summary

The approach of this chapter is empirical and inductive. In it, the observed Danish wage distribution data and the job separations model estimated by Christensen et al. (2001) are shown to be inconsistent with the hypothesis that the observed hourly wage rates actually paid by those firms located in the left tail of the wage distribution are chosen to maximize expected employer profit. However, the distribution of wages paid and firm sizes observed in the Danish IDA can be interpreted as the outcome of a bilateral bargain between each worker-employer pair after they meet. Furthermore, the inferred productivity probability density function is identified by the job separation flows and the wage and size distributions observed. Although the model and the data imply that productivity across employers is unimodal, it is also highly right skewed with the most productive 1 percent employing over half of the workers in the Danish private sector.

To conclude, the Danish IDA data are consistent with the hypothesis that wages are set through decentralized bilateral bargaining but contradict the hypothesis that they maximize employer profit as proposed by Burdett and Mortensen (1998). Of course, this outcome need not hold in other economies. Moreover, most of the qualitative implications of the model with bilateral bargaining are the same as those of the original Burdett-Mortensen model. For example, more productive firms pay a higher wage and invest more in recruiting effort. Wage dispersion reflects differences in employer productivity, and workers move from low to high productivity firms as a consequence. The inference that most workers are employed by the most productive employers suggests that the market, though imperfect in several senses, may allocate labor among firms reasonably efficiently.

Notes

1. Koning et al. (2000) come to a similar conclusion using IDA data for individual workers for a different time period. Specifically, they test and reject restrictions that the monopsony model imposes on a standard wage equation regression.

2. Unemployed search is viewed as the relevant outside option in the bargaining problem whether or not the worker is employed when they meet in this formulation. One defense of the assumption is that unemployed search is the only immediately available outside option once a worker accepts employment. In other words, past employment experience is not relevant in any future renegotiation of the wage.

3. The argument used in the proof of Proposition 2 in chapter 1 applies in both cases.

4. These estimates are slightly different from those reported in Christiansen et al. (2001) because they were obtained using a different bin width for the construction of the wage and offer c.d.f.s', F and G. Otherwise, the estimates were obtained using the same procedure.

5. More recently, Frederiksen and Westergaard-Nielsen (2002) report that 9.05 percent of separations end in transitions to no job on average over the entire 1980–1990 IDA sample period. They also find that the overall separation rates were above average in 1994.

6. For an earlier classic history of the Danish labor relations system, see Galenson (1952).

7. Of course, the graph of $w(p)$ will have a similar shape as that depicted in figure 4.3 for the monopsony case when $\beta = 0$. Hence, by continuity, the monotonicity of $w(p)$ does not hold for all β sufficiently small. But in our case, computation results verify that monotonicity does hold for all $\beta \geq 0.05$.

5   The Wage-Tenure Relation

5.1   Introduction

In the versions of all the models considered so far, wages are invariant over the duration of a job match by assumption. The specification is at odds with two kinds of empirical evidence. First, employment contracts that condition pay on length of service with an employer are not uncommon. An initial probation period after which the employer makes a formal decision to continue the relationship into the future is almost generic. If the decision is positive, the worker usually receives a raise and/or promotion. More generally, there is an expectation that promotions and higher wages will come with tenure on most jobs. Finally, the estimated coefficient on a job-tenure variable in a standard wage equation is always positive. The purpose of this chapter is to review recent attempts to explain the wage-tenure relation in generalizations of the Burdett-Mortensen framework.

The interpretation of tenure effects in wage equations is a subject of considerable controversy.[1] Human capital theorists argue that returns to tenure reflect increases in match-specific productivity while others emphasize the incentive effects of a positively sloped wage-tenure profile. A third group suggests that the measured tenure effect in wage equations is primarily the consequence of sample selection induced by a rent-seeking job search. The theories presented in this chapter fall into the latter two traditions.

If on-the-job wage growth were attributable to causes outside the scope of the strategic competition embodied in the Burdett-Mortensen model, it could easily be allowed for in the analysis. However, a purely theoretical critique of the assumed flat wage-tenure profile specification also exists. Namely, if an employer has monopsony power in the sense that marginal revenue product exceeds the wage, then she incurs a loss of future rents when an employee quits to take another job. Rather than accept the loss, the employer has an incentive to respond by matching the outside offer, at least up to the point of being indifferent to the separation. In short, a quit is not generally a jointly efficient separation in the model as specified. Below I show that a counteroffer strategy of this form will break the constant wage Burdett-Mortensen solution in a game that allows for more general compensation schemes.

In papers by Postel-Vinay and Robin (1999, 2001), employers are assumed to make counteroffers when an employee generates an outside offer. All employers pay workers hired from unemployment their reservation wage but compete with any alternative employer that the worker meets subsequently. When an employed worker has an outside employment opportunity, the employer offering the alternative job and the worker's current employer bid against each other until the expected future value of either hiring or keeping the worker is zero for one of the two. If the productivity of the worker with the current employer exceeds that with the alternative, the worker stays but is paid a wage equal to his productivity in the alternative job. Otherwise, the worker quits to take the outside offer at a wage that equalizes the value of continued employment with the value of alternative employment. In either case, the separation outcome is efficient and the worker's subsequent wage is determined by the outcome of a "second price auction" involving the current employer and a prospective alternative.

Wage dispersion exists when counteroffers are allowed both within and across employing firms. Furthermore, wages are positively correlated with both job tenure and experience. Because the higher wage can only be obtained once employed, an unemployed worker is willing to accept and will be offered a wage below the opportunity cost of employment to "get a foot in the door." Once employed, the worker either receives raises or moves to a more productive employer in response to outside employment opportunities as they arise. Although the worker is generally willing to take a pay cut to make such a move, that willingness is justified by the expectations that the new employer is able and willing to make even larger counteroffers in the future. Hence, the approach provides a rich theory of both interfirm and intrafirm wage differences.

Postel-Vinay and Robin (2001) use the model and observed wage dispersion both across and within firms in France to identify the relative contribution of worker fixed effects, employer heterogeneity, and job search to wage dispersion. Interestingly, they find little role for unobserved worker ability as an explanation for dispersion except for the occupations requiring the most education and cognitive ability.

Although the counteroffer wage determination strategy has a certain appeal, problems exist with the specification as a wage determination rule. Unlike in the market for academic economists in the United States, making counteroffers is not the norm in many labor markets. More typically, a worker who informs his employer of a more lucrative outside option is first congratulated and then asked to clear out immediately.

There are several possible reasons for this alternative outcome. One is asymmetric information. How can a worker convince his employer that he has an outside offer let alone credibly communicate its terms? Certainly the mere threat to quit has no force. Only the act of accepting the alternative is credible. But then it is typically too late for the former employer to make a convincing counteroffer. Of course, the alternative employer can communicate the terms of the offer, but what incentive is there for her to do so? At best such behavior only increases the wage she will have to pay. Furthermore, communication between the worker's current and prospective employer could generate collusion between the two at the expense of the worker in the auction that is supposed to determine the new wage. Finally, offer matching generates interfirm wage differences that are not obviously justified. Workers view raises gained in this way by those regarded as equals as returns to "luck" rather than ability or effort. Morale problems are often cited as reasons against this form of wage dispersion.

Moral hazard is another reason why a firm may choose not to match outside offers. In the absence of costless monitoring of search activity, the employees of a firm offering to match outside offers will be encouraged by the policy to find them. This behavior will increase both the likelihood of future raises and the separations. For both reasons, it may be more profitable for the employer to commit to a strategy of not responding to outside offers even though doing so is time consistent.[2]

For these reasons, Stevens (1999) argues that employers typically offer take-it-or-leave-it wage-tenure contracts instead of matching outside offers. However, the optimal wage-tenure profile will not be constant when both worker and employer are risk neutral as assumed by Burdett and Mortensen. Indeed, an obvious optimal contract, one that also generates efficient turnover, specifies that the worker "buys" the job upfront with an appropriate side payment and then receives the value of his marginal productivity thereafter. Many have argued that capital market restrictions prevent workers from borrowing against future labor income and, consequently, severely limit contracts of this form. Even so, Stevens shows that any two-tier wage contract, one in which a low but positive initial wage is paid for some fixed period of time after which the wage is set equal to the value of marginal product, is also a noncooperative equilibrium to the contract offer game. When all workers and jobs are identical, contracts of this form also prevent inefficient separation.

Identical employers all offer the same contract in equilibrium in the Stevens model, and in that sense there is no cross-employer wage dispersion. Still, equilibrium wage behavior in her model looks very much like that obtained in the Postel-Vinay–Robin model, at least in the case of identical workers and jobs. Namely, after the fixed "probation period," an employed worker earns a value of marginal product while during the probation period each earns some lower wage. As a consequence, interfirm wage dispersion does exist and is perfectly correlated with tenure. Again, the worker is willing to accept a wage less than the unemployment benefit. Indeed, if the initial wage equates the value of unemployment to the initial value of employment, then the only difference between the two models is that the length of the probation period in the former is a random variable rather than a deterministic number.

Burdett and Coles (2001) add an interesting and important new twist to the analysis by investigating the effects of a borrowing constraint and risk aversion on the nature of the wage-tenure contract. Specifically, they assume that workers have time-separable preferences for smooth consumption streams and cannot borrow on future labor income. Hence, if unemployed workers have no liquid assets, risk-neutral employers face a trade-off between the moral hazard problem implicit in the workers' decision to seek a better job and their ability to provide the worker with a smooth consumption stream. In short, no turnover and complete income insurance, the two conditions required for first best when workers and jobs are respectively identical, are in conflict. As a consequence of the tension between these two goals, the authors show that the constrained optimal wage-tenure contract is a smooth increasing function.

So the Burdett-Coles model implies intrafirm wage dispersion associated with differences in tenure. In addition, interfirm dispersion exist for the same reason as in the original Burdett-Mortensen model. Specifically, only a mixed strategy equilibrium exists in which identical employers offer different contracts all of which yield a common expected future profit. Interesting, cross-employer differentials boil down to dispersion in initial wage offers where each value represents a different starting point on what the authors call a common *baseline salary scale*. Otherwise, the distributions of both wages offered across vacancies and wages earned by employed workers are very similar to those implied by the original Burdett-Mortensen model. In short, the basic insight survives.

5.2   Sequential Auctions

Consider an employer who finds herself in a market characterized by the fixed-wage contract solution to the Burdett-Mortensen model. Can she offer an acceptable alternative compensation scheme that would yield a greater expected profit than any of the continuum of optimal fixed-wage contracts? Because the wage needed to attract an unemployed worker is different from that required to retain him, the answer is yes.

Suppose that some employer were to offer a "two-tiered" wage scheme composed of an initial wage equal to the lower support of the Burdett-Mortensen fixed-wage equilibrium solution, $\underline{w}$, together with the promise to pay the highest wage offered by any of the other employers, $\overline{w}$, in the event that the worker receives an outside offer. Recall that, $\underline{w} = b$ and $b < \overline{w} < p$. As the expected present value of the income stream offered by this contract exceeds that obtained by accepting employment with the firm offering to pay the lowest fixed wage, equal to the common reservation wage, the offered income stream is clearly acceptable to an unemployed worker. Hence, all we need show is that the expected profit of offering this deviation exceeds the expected profit of pursuing a fixed-wage strategy given that the distribution of other offers is the Burdett-Mortensen solution.

The value of hiring a worker under the proposed alternative payment scheme, denoted as $\widehat{J}$, solves the following continuous-time Bellman equation

$$r\widehat{J} = p - b - \delta\widehat{J} + \lambda[J(\overline{w}) - \widehat{J}],$$

where as previously δ is the job destruction rate, λ is the offer arrival rate,

$$J(w) = (p - w)/(r + d(w))$$

is the value of continuation under a fixed-wage offer of w, and

$$d(w) = \delta + \lambda[1 - F(w)].$$

is the job separation rate.[3] The equal profit condition in the Burdett-Mortensen model implies that the offer distribution F is such that

$$\pi = h(w)J(w) = uJ(b) = \left(\frac{\delta}{\delta + \lambda}\right)\left(\frac{p - b}{r + \delta + \lambda}\right) \quad \text{for all } w \in [b, \overline{w}],$$

where

$$u = \delta/(\delta + \lambda)$$

is the steady-state unemployment rate and

$$h(w) = (\delta + \lambda G(w))/(\delta + \lambda)$$

is the probability that a worker chosen at random will accept the fixed-wage offer w in a Burdett-Mortensen equilibrium. Because the expected profit of offering the deviation satisfies $\widehat{\pi} \geq u\widehat{J}$[4], $\pi = h(\overline{w})J(\overline{w})$ from the equal profit condition, and $h(\overline{w}) = 1$, the following inequality implies that the Burdett-Mortensen solution is not an equilibrium of a game that allows employers to offer more general compensation packages:

$$\widehat{\pi} \geq u\widehat{J} = u\left(\frac{p - b + \lambda J(\overline{w})}{r + \delta + \lambda}\right) = u\left(\frac{p - b + \lambda\pi}{r + \delta + \lambda}\right)$$

$$= \left(1 + \frac{\delta\lambda}{(\delta + \lambda)(r + \delta + \lambda)}\right)\pi > \pi.$$

5.2.1 Homogenous Productivity

Although the deviant contract is more profitable when all the other employers pay the same wage to all workers, it is not an equilibrium solution to the more general game in which counteroffers are permitted. Indeed, the employer who is attempting to poach the worker has an incentive to pay more than $\overline{w}$ since it is strictly less than the worker's productivity. Postel-Vinay and Robin (1999) resolve this problem by supposing that the two employers engage in a Bertrand bidding war resulting in a new wage for the worker equal to p. Equivalently, the worker is viewed as conducting a sealed bid second price auction to determine his wage. But now, the initial wage offered to an unemployed worker must actually be lower than the unemployment benefit if offering it is more profitable than the fixed-wage offer $w = b$.

Let w_0 represent the initial wage offered. Given the anticipated outcome of the auction that takes place when a employee obtains an outside offer in the future, namely, that his wage will be bid to $w = p$, the worker's value of employment given an initial wage w_0, denoted again as $W(w)$ for simplicity, now solves

$$r W(w_0) = w_0 + \delta(U - W(w_0)) + \lambda[W(p) - W(w_0)], \qquad (5.1)$$

where $W(p) = (p + \delta U)/(r + \delta)$ is the solution to the same equation given $w_0 = p$. The associated value of hiring the worker to the employer, denoted $J(w)$, solves

$$r J(w_0) = p - w_0 - \delta J(w_0) + \lambda[J(p) - J(w_0)], \qquad (5.2)$$

where, of course, $J(p) = 0$.

As specified earlier, an employer ends up offering $w = p$ if the applicant is employed and $w = w_0$ if unemployed. Because the unemployed will accept any offer not less than the reservation wage, the unique initial wage offered by all employers is the reservation wage $w_0 = R$ defined by $W(R) = U$. Because the value of unemployment solves

$$r U = b + \lambda[W(w_0) - U], \qquad (5.3)$$

and

$$W(R) = \frac{R + \delta U + \lambda W(p)}{r + \delta + \lambda} = \frac{R + \delta U + \lambda \left(\frac{p + \delta U}{r + \delta} \right)}{r + \delta + \lambda} = \frac{b}{r} = U,$$

the initial wage offered and accepted by any unemployed worker

$$w_0 = R = b - \frac{\lambda(p - b)}{r + \delta} \qquad (5.4)$$

is less than the unemployment benefit. Of course, this result is a consequence of the fact that the worker can earn the higher wage $w = p$ only after an initial spell earning the initial wage $w = R$. He is willing to accept an initial wage less than the unemployment benefit in order to get his foot in the door.

Although employed workers are eventually paid a competitive wage, they initially receive less than the unemployment benefit. Indeed, because the total expected pay during the initial period is

$$\frac{b - R}{\lambda} = \frac{p - b}{r + \delta},$$

the difference between the unemployment benefit and earnings over the expected duration of the initial period is exactly equal to the present value of the total rent accruing to any match, the term $(p - b)/(r + \delta)$. In other words, each worker effectively "pays for the job" at least on average by accepting a sufficiently low initial wage.

Of course, this simple compensation strategy will induce a positive tenure effect in wage observations. Since the probability that an outside offer will arrive within the tenure period $(0, t]$ is $1 - e^{-\lambda t}$, the average wage received by a sample of workers who have attained tenure t,

$$w(t) = (1 - e^{-\lambda t})p + e^{-\lambda t}R = R + (p - R)(1 - e^{-\lambda t}),$$

increases with t and has a concave shape as typically observed in the data. However, this relation only holds on average and, consequently, observationally identical workers are still paid differently in the equilibrium even conditional on t. But, even to the extent that wage differences are associated with tenure difference, the workers are nevertheless identical. Consequently, all wage differences implied by the model represent pure dispersion as originally defined.

5.2.2 Productive Heterogeneity

When employer productivity differs, Postel-Vinay and Robin (1999) argue that a worker moves in response to an outside offer only if the poacher is more productive since the current employer will only bid up to its firm-specific labor productivity. Even if the worker does not move, the wage paid rises as a consequence of the auction between the two contestant employers if the worker is currently paid less than the productivity of the prospective poacher. In short, an individual's wage path evolves over time as the outcome of a series of "second price" auctions that take place sequentially as the worker is contacted by a series of employers. Intrafirm wage dispersion is generated by this sequential auction process. Differences in wages earned by two different employees of the same firm reflect differences in the two workers' labor market experiences. However, "experience" does not augment an individual worker's own productivity directly. Instead, workers with experience command higher wages in expectation because they are more likely to have been employed by a more productive firm in the past.

In a market equilibrium of this form, the value of employment depends on the productivity of the employer as well as the wage earned. When unemployed the reservation wage conditional on the employer's productivity, denoted $R_0(p)$, solves

$$W(R_0(p), p) = U, \tag{5.5}$$

where $W(w, p)$ is the value of employment at a firm of productivity p when earning a wage w and U is the value of unemployment. Since every employer pays an unemployed worker her reservation wage, the flow value of unemployment is the unemployment benefit, namely,

$$rU = b + \lambda \int [\max \langle W(R_0(x), x), U \rangle - U] d\Gamma(x) = b, \tag{5.6}$$

where $\Gamma(p)$ is the fraction of employers with productivity p or less.

Since a worker's current employer will pay up to the worker's productivity, p, to retain her, an alternative employer, one of productivity p', must offer a wage greater than $R(p', p)$ where

$$W(R(p, p'), p') = W(p, p). \tag{5.7}$$

Any smaller offer is matched by the former employer. Now, if $W(w, p)$ is increasing in both its arguments as one should expect, then $R(p, p') \geq p'$ if the alternative employer is less productive than the current one, that is, $p' \leq p$. Although a less productive poacher cannot afford to offer a wage that will attract the worker as a consequence, the worker must receive a new wage no less than $R(p', p)$, that which makes him indifferent between employment with her current employer and the alternative, if his current w is less. Hence, the worker stays but receives a raise from the worker's current employer if and only if the productivity of the prospective employer satisfies $p \geq p' \geq q(w, p)$, where

$$R(q(w, p), p) = w. \tag{5.8}$$

In sum, the worker stays but receives a raise equal to $R(p', p)$ if $p \geq p' \geq q(w, p)$ and moves and is paid a new wage equal to $R(p, p')$ if $p > p'$. Hence, the value of employment function solves

$$rW(w, p) = w + \lambda \int_{q(w,p)}^{p} [W(R(x, p), p) - W(w, p)] d\Gamma(x) \tag{5.9}$$

$$+ \lambda[1 - \Gamma(p)][W(p, p) - W(w, p)] + \delta[U - W(w, p)]$$

because (5.7) holds when $p' > p$.

Since $R(p, p) = p$ from (5.7), equation (5.8) requires $q(p, p) = p$. Because the same two equations imply $q(R(p, p'), p') = p$ and $W(R(x, p'), p') = W(x, x)$,

$$(r + \delta)W(p, p) = p + \delta U = (r + \delta)\, W(R(p, p'), p')$$

$$= R(p, p') + \delta U + \lambda \int_p^{p'} [W(x, x) - W(p, p)]\, d\Gamma(x)$$

from equation (5.9). Since $W(x, x) = \frac{x + \delta U}{r + \delta}$ from the first equality, integration by parts yields the following solution for the outside offer required to move the worker from an employer of type p to one of productivity $p' > p$:

$$R(p, p') = p - \frac{\lambda}{r + \delta} \int_p^{p'} [1 - \Gamma(x)]\, dx. \tag{5.10}$$

As corollaries,

$$R_0(p) = R(b, p) \tag{5.11}$$

from (5.5) and (5.6), and

$$q(w, p) - \frac{\lambda}{r + \delta} \int_{q(w, p)}^p [1 - \Gamma(x)]\, dx = w \tag{5.12}$$

from (5.8).

It follows that the productivities of an employed worker's current and former employer are sufficient statistics for the current wage earned, that is,

$$w = R(q, p) = q - \frac{\lambda}{r + \delta} \int_q^p [1 - \Gamma(x)]\, dx, \tag{5.13}$$

where q is the productivity of the former employer if hired from another firm and $q = b$ otherwise, and p is the productivity of the worker's current employer. Although the wage increases with the productivity of the former employer, it decreases with p because there is an option value of being employed by a more productive employer. Indeed, as $W(R(q, p), p) = W(q, q)$ by definition, the worker is willing to take an implicit pay cut equal to the difference between the wage the former employer is willing to pay, q, and w to move to a more productive employer with productivity $p > q$. The difference is the value of the prospective raise received in response to the next outside offer given employment with the more productive employer. Relative to the forgone wage q, the prospective raise is $x - q$ where x is the productivity of the next employer met provided that x lies in the interval between p and q. Indeed, because

$$\lambda \Pr\{q < x \leq p\}E\left\{\frac{x-q}{r+\delta}\bigg| q < x \leq p\right\} = \frac{\lambda}{r+\delta}\int_q^p (x-q)\,d\Gamma(x)$$

$$= \frac{\lambda}{r+\delta}\int_q^p [1 - \Gamma(x)]\,dx = q - w,$$

the value of the option is the expected difference in the values of the next raise obtained given employment with a more productive firm.

For an unemployed worker, the difference between the initial productivity contingent wage offer,

$$w_0(p) = R_0(p) = R(b, p) = b - \frac{\lambda}{r+\delta}\int_b^p [1 - \Gamma(x)]\,dx, \tag{5.14}$$

and the unemployment benefit, b, is the price an unemployed worker is willing to pay for the opportunity to attain the first wrung of the job ladder. The implicit price is higher the more productive is the worker's first employer for the reason already reviewed. In other words, less productive employers must pay higher initial wages. This outcome is a consequence of the fact that workers are willing to trade a higher wage level now for the better prospect of future wage growth offered by employment with a more productive firm. In sum, the worker indifference condition (5.7) implies that more productive firms offer a lower starting wage but a steeper implicit expected wage-tenure profile in any labor market equilibrium.

5.2.3 The Equilibrium Wage Distribution
The unconditional probability that a worker earns a wage of w or less is given by

$$G(w) = \int G(w|p)\,dL(p), \tag{5.15}$$

where $G(w|p)$ is the productivity contingent infrafirm wage c.d.f. and $L(p)$ is fraction of employed workers who work for firms with productivity p or less. These two cumulative distribution functions can be derived as the solutions to worker flow equations as in the previous models.

Since the transition rate from unemployment to employment is λ and from employment to unemployment is δ, the steady-state unemployment rate is again

$$u = \frac{\delta}{\delta + \lambda}. \tag{5.16}$$

Because the flow into the stock of workers employed by firms with productivity p or less is simply $\lambda \Gamma(p)u$ while the flow out of the same stock is $(\delta + \lambda[1 - \Gamma(p)])(1 - u)L(p)$, the equality of the two generate the following steady-state solution for the fraction employed by firms of productivity p or less:

$$L(p) = \frac{\lambda \Gamma(p)u}{(\delta + \lambda[1 - \Gamma(p)])(1 - u)} = \frac{\delta \Gamma(p)}{\delta + \lambda[1 - \Gamma(p)]}. \tag{5.17}$$

Given employment in a firm of productivity type p, workers earning w or less leave either as a consequence of layoff or because they receive an offer from a firm with productivity $p' > q(w, p)$. Workers flowing into the same category are new hires who were either unemployed or employed by a firm with productivity $p' \leq q(w, p)$. Equating the flows yields

$$(\delta + \lambda[1 - \Gamma(q(w, p))])(1 - u)L'(p)G(w|p)$$

$$= (\lambda u + \lambda(1 - u)L(q(w, p)))\Gamma'(p)$$

where, of course, $L'(p)$ and $\Gamma'(p)$ are the density of workers employed at and the density of offers made by firms with productivity p, respectively, and $G(w|p)$ represents the conditional distribution of wages over workers employed in firms of productivity p. This equation together with equations (5.16) and (5.17) imply that intrafirm wage dispersion can be represented in terms of the following conditional distribution:

$$\begin{aligned} G(w|p) &= \left(\frac{\lambda u + \lambda(1 - u)L(q(w, p))}{(\delta + \lambda[1 - \Gamma(q(w, p))])(1 - u)}\right)\left(\frac{\Gamma'(p)}{L'(p)}\right) \\ &= \left(\frac{\delta + \lambda L(q(w, p))}{\delta + \lambda[1 - \Gamma(q(w, p))]}\right)\left(\frac{(\delta + \lambda[1 - \Gamma(p)])^2}{\delta(\delta + \lambda)}\right) \\ &= \left(\frac{\delta + \lambda[1 - \Gamma(p)]}{\delta + \lambda[1 - \Gamma(q(w, p))]}\right)^2 \end{aligned} \tag{5.18}$$

given equation (5.16).

The support of the productivity contingent within firm wage distribution is $[R(b, p), p]$. Since $q(R(b, p), p) = b$, this distribution has a mass point at its lower support equal to

$$G(R(b, p)|p) = \left(\frac{\delta + \lambda[1 - \Gamma(p)]}{\delta + \lambda[1 - \Gamma(b)]} \right)^2,$$

which is the fraction of employees hired from unemployment by a firm of type p. Although this fraction remains positive, the fact that $L(p) \to 0$ for all $p < \overline{p}$ and $R(b, \overline{p}) \to \overline{p}$ as $\delta/\lambda \to 0$ implies that every worker is employed by a firm of the most productive type and receives a wage equal to her marginal productivity in the limit as friction vanishes. In other words, this model shares the Burdett-Mortensen implication that the market equilibrium limits to the perfectly competitive case as search friction vanishes.

5.2.4 Empirical Inference

Postel-Vinay and Robin (2001) use the model to decompose the variance of log wages found in the French Déclarations Annuelles des Données Sociales (DADs) panel data into worker and employer fixed effects and a random effect attributable to search friction. Although worker abilities differ in their version of the model, they argue that these are independent of employer productivity for reasons that were pointed out in chapters 1 and 2. By assumption, a worker's productivity when employed is $p\varepsilon$ where p is firm specific and ε represents the contribution of a worker's ability, and the opportunity cost of employment is $b\varepsilon$ in Postel-Vinay and Robin's generalization of the model developed earlier.[5] In this case, the variance of worker' log wages can be expressed as

$$Var \ln w = E\, Var(\ln w|p) + Var E\,(\ln w|p)$$

$$= Var \ln \varepsilon + Var E\,(\ln w|p) + (E\, Var(\ln w|p) - Var \ln \varepsilon)$$

$$= Var \ln \varepsilon + Var E\,[\ln R(q, p)|p] + E\, Var[\ln R(q, p)|p], \qquad (5.19)$$

where ε represents the worker fixed effect that is orthogonal to p in equilibrium in the model. The first term then is the contribution of the worker fixed effect to the total variance of the log wage. Because the second term represents the contribution of employer heterogeneity in productivity to the log wage variance while the third term is the contribution of within firm variance in wages not due to heterogeneity in ability, they interpret them as the contributions of the firm effect and of market friction, respectively.

Table 5.1
Log wage variance decomposition

Occupation	$E \ln w$	$Var \ln w$	Worker effect (%)	Firm effect (%)	Friction effect (%)
Managers and engineers	4.81	0.180	41.9	19.4	38.7
Supervisors	4.28	0.125	17.8	27.9	55.1
Technicians	4.31	0.077	6.6	32.8	60.6
Administrative support	4.00	0.082	9.7	34.6	55.7
Skilled manual	4.05	0.069	0	41.5	58.5
Sales and service	3.74	0.050	5.0	37.1	57.9
Unskilled manual	3.77	0.057	0	40.8	59.2

Source: Postel-Vinay and Robin (2001), Table 7.

Using the structure of the model outlined previously, Postel-Vinay and Robin (2001) obtain estimates of the second and third components on the right side and derive the contribution of the worker fixed effect as a residual. They do so for each of seven subsamples defined by worker occupation. The decomposition results for the case of the simple expected wealth maximizing assumption are summarized in table 5.1. They are quite remarkable.

First, differences in worker ability is an important explanation of wage dispersion only for managers and engineers. Indeed, for manual workers, whether skilled or not, worker heterogeneity contributes not at all to wage differences. Second, within firm variation attributed to search friction is the most important direct explanation for wage dispersion in all occupations other than managers and engineers where even there it runs a close second to the contribution of heterogeneity in ability. Finally, as the authors point out, their results are derived from almost the same data studied by Abowd, Finer, and Kramarz (1999) and Abowd and Kramarz (2000a,b). Since the Postel-Vinay–Robin (2001) results account for the selection effects implied by search, they suggest that the contribution of the worker effect obtained in these papers is a large overestimate of the contribution of unobserved worker heterogeneity to industry differentials.

5.3 Wage-Tenure Contracts

5.3.1 Risk-Neutral Workers
The general empirical plausibility of a counteroffer equilibrium is questionable. First, its implementation requires symmetric information about

an applicant's employment status and every employee's outside options. Second, it generates interfirm wage differentials across observably equivalent workers who violate equity norms. Third, an employer's ability to capture all of match rent requires that the worker be able to finance his purchase of the job implicit in the low and possibly negative wage received during the initial employment period prior to the arrival of an outside offer. For these reasons, Stevens (1999) suggests that employers offer a long-term tenure-contingent contract on a take-it-or-leave-it basis. She shows that equilibrium contracts of this form also eliminate inefficient separation and extract all of the match rent. As it turns out, the form of the contract looks very much like the average wage path generated by the counteroffer strategy.

A wage-tenure contract specifies the wage paid as a function only of actual tenure attained in a specific job-worker match. Let the function $w(t)$ defined on the positive reals represent such a contract where t is tenure. Consider a contract of the following form: Pay $w(t) = w_0$ for all $t < T$ and $w = w_1$ thereafter. Suppose that all workers and employers are respectively identical and all employers offer the same contract. Any such contract, characterized by the triple (w_0, w_1, T), has a continuation value to the worker denoted as $W(t)$. Since no worker will move from one employer to another under these assumptions, the continuation value is the particular forward solution to the linear differential equation

$$rW - \frac{dW}{dt} = w_0 + \delta[U - W(t)] \tag{5.20}$$

on the interval $[0, T]$ that satisfies the terminal condition

$$W(T) = \frac{w_1 + \delta U}{r + \delta}, \tag{5.21}$$

where dW/dt represent pure capital gain associated with the passage of time under the contract and $W(T)$ is the expected present value of the contract at every tenure greater than or equal to T. Since the steady-state solution to the linear differential equation (5.20) is unstable and equal to $(w_0 + \delta U)/(r + \delta)$, one can show that the only solution consistent with the boundary condition has property that $W(t)$ is strictly increasing in tenure if and only if $w_1 > w_0$.

Consider the contract identified by (R, p, T) where $w_1 = p$ is the common value of worker productivity and $w_0 = R$ is the reservation wage, the solution to $W(0) = U$. Because

$$rU = b + \lambda[W(0) - U], \tag{5.22}$$

it follows that R solves

$$W(0) = \left[\int_0^T (w_0 + \delta U) e^{-(r+\delta)s} \, ds + e^{-(r+\delta)T} W(T) \right]$$

$$= \left(1 - e^{-(r+\delta)T}\right) \left(\frac{R + \delta U}{r + \delta} \right) + e^{-(r+\delta)T} \left(\frac{p + \delta U}{r + \delta} \right) = U = \frac{b}{r}$$

by integration and equation (5.21). Hence, one can express the initial wage as

$$w_0 = R = b - \frac{p - b}{e^{(r+\delta)T} - 1} \approx b - \frac{p - b}{(r + \delta)T} \tag{5.23}$$

when $(r + \delta)T$ is small. Note the analogy to equation (5.4) that defines the reservation wage in the counteroffer equilibrium given that all firms are equally productive. Under this contract, the worker again "pays for the job" by accepting the low wage R for an initial period of deterministic length T.

Finally, any such contract is a dominant strategy solution to a wage-tenure contract offer game. First, no worker once employed will look for alternative employment because the value of starting over with another employer $W(0)$ is strictly less than the value of continuing $W(t)$ with his current employer given any contract of the specified form. Because the joint surplus value of any job-worker match is maximized and the employer receives all of the value, which is $J(0) = (p-b)/(r+\delta)$, there exists no other contract that can do better. Indeed, because workers care only about the expected present value of the contract, there is a continuum of equilibria of this kind, each associated with a different value of T even if $w_0 = R$ is constrained to be nonnegative as already noted.

5.3.2   Risk-Averse Workers

The demonstration that the perfectly discriminating monopsony outcome can be rationalized as noncooperative equilibrium behavior in their environment while a fixed-wage contract is not an equilibrium represents a serious challenge to the Burdett-Mortensen analysis. However, this outcome is very sensitive to the assumption that workers care only about the expected present value of future wage payments. Burdett and Coles (2001) show that a little bit of risk aversion restores the basic insight in the sense that again identical employers offer different contracts in equilibrium. In addition, the fact that their generalization also implies a positively sloped wage-tenure schedule is a bonus that addresses the empirical objection to the Burdett-Mortensen fixed-wage assumption. Indeed, the generalized model offers still another explanation for the tenure effect on wages.

A clear way to see the difference between Stevens's analysis and that of Coles and Burdett is to realize that a risk-averse worker without access to a perfect capital market strongly prefers a constant income stream to a two-tier wage structure of the same expected present value. However, if there are differences in the value of the contracts offered by employers, then employees have an incentive to quit once an alternative employer offering a more valuable contract is encountered. Because a higher quit probability reduces the employer's expected surplus, a trade-off exists between the worker's desire for a smooth income stream and the employer's incentive to reduce quits. Since no wage-tenure contract exists that can fully accomplish both goals, the result is a tenure-contingent wage that is relatively flat but increasing.

Of course, this observation presumes that the contracts offered have different worker values even though employers are identical. Burdett and Coles prove that any equilibrium will have this property for precisely the same reasons that identical firms offer different wages in the original Burdett-Mortensen model. First, they show that any wage-tenure contract that is optimal from the employer point of view given that their employee's outside options can be characterized by a continuous distribution of contract value offers defined on a compact convex support belongs to a one-parameter family of contracts. That parameter can be viewed as the common value of each contract in the family to the workers. Second, they show that a unique continuous distribution of contract values to the workers defined on a compact convex support exists with the property that the expected profit of offering all contracts in the family are equal and exceed the expected profit of any other feasible contract offer.

5.3.3   Optimal Wage-Tenure Contracts

Workers are assumed to be identical, risk averse, and liquidity constrained in the sense that borrowing on their future labor income is not possible. Under these conditions, each worker desires a smooth consumption stream but cannot finance it. Indeed, if offered a wage contract that grows with tenure as will be true in equilibrium, the worker's best option is to consume all of his current income given no initial wealth. This outcome in assumed in the rest of the book.

Let $u(y)$ represent instantaneous utility of income where $y = b$, the unemployment benefit, when unemployed and $y = w$, wage income, when employed. By assumption, $u(y)$ is increasing and twice differentiable with $u''(y) < 0$. Prospective future income streams are ranked according to their expected present value of the future utility flow where the parameter ρ represents the common worker rate of time preference. Hence, given a future generally stochastic income process $\{y(t)\}_0^\infty$ where $y(t)$ is income at future time t, its utility value is represented by the usual expected value integral

$$E_0 \int_0^\infty u(y(t))e^{-\rho t}\,dt, \tag{5.24}$$

where E_0 represents the expectation operator take with respect to information available at $t = 0$.

The productivity of every worker on any job is the same and denoted as p. The worker's continuation value of a contract, represented by the contingent wage sequence $\vec{w} = \{w(s)\}_t^\infty$, at tenure t, denoted $W(t; \vec{w})$, is equal to the expected future stream of utility given that the worker acts to maximize value in the future. A contract is acceptable if its initial value $W_0 = W(0, \vec{w})$ exceeds the value of unemployment denoted by U. Burdett and Coles (2001) seek a labor market equilibrium with the following properties:

A1: If acceptable initially, the contract is also acceptable at future tenure dates, that is, $W(0, \vec{w}) \geq U \Rightarrow W(t, \vec{w}) \geq U$ for all tenure $t \geq 0$.

A2: The distribution of initial contract values, represented by the c.d.f. $F(W)$, is continuous and differentiable, with positive density on the interior of its support $[\underline{W}, \overline{W}]$.

A3: All contracts offered are acceptable, that is, $\underline{W} \geq U$, and the best contract is less valuable to a worker than the fixed-wage contract $w(t) = p$, that is, $\overline{W} < (u(p) + \delta U)/(\rho + \delta)$.

The authors first derive an employer's best response wage-tenure contract under the assumption that the contracts offered by all the other employers satisfy these three conditions. Workers receive offers at Poisson rate λ, these are random draws from the distribution of contract values $F(W)$, and existing matches are hit by a destruction shock at Poisson rate δ. Because the worker's optimal decision is to accept a more valuable outside contract whenever the opportunity arises, the value function

$W = W(t, \vec{w})$ solves the following continuous-time Bellman equation:

$$\rho W - \frac{dW}{dt} = u(w(t)) + \delta[U - W] + \lambda \int_{W}^{\overline{W}} [x - W] d F(x) \qquad (5.25)$$

given assumption A1 where ρ is the workers' common rate of time discount.

As a worker accepts the first offer with value greater than U, the value of unemployment is the solution to

$$\rho U = u(b) + \lambda \int_{U}^{\overline{W}} [x - U] d F(x). \qquad (5.26)$$

Similarly, the continuation value at tenure t of the contract to an employer, denoted $J = J(t, \vec{w})$, satisfies the following Bellman equation:

$$r J - \frac{dJ}{dt} = p - w(t) - (\delta + \lambda[1 - F(W)]) J, \qquad (5.27)$$

where r is the interest rate and $\delta + \lambda[1 - F(W)]$ is the match separation rate.

Burdett and Coles regard a contract as a commitment to a wage policy with terms that can be enforced in the future. However, workers are free to move from one employer to another in accord with a time-consistent optimal acceptance strategy. In particular, an *optimal wage-tenure contract* maximizes the expected present value of the future profit accruing to a match given the initial value of the contract offered to any worker. Formally, it is the solution to the constrained problem

$$\Pi(W_0) \equiv \max_{\vec{w}} J(0, \vec{w}) = \max_{\vec{w}} \int_{0}^{\infty} [p - w(t)] e^{- \int_{0}^{t} [r + \delta + \lambda(1 - F(W(s, \vec{w})))] ds} \, dt$$

$$(5.28)$$

subject to

$$W(0; \vec{w}) \geq W_0,$$

where $J(0, \vec{w})$ is the forward solution to (5.27) at $t = 0$ for any given wage-tenure contract and W_0 represents the initial value of the contract to the worker. Because the solution to this variational problem need not maximize the employer's continuation value of the match for positive values of t, the problem is not a standard one in dynamic programming.

Burdett and Coles (2001) establish that the family of optimal contracts associated with the parameter W_0 has all the following properties: First, since a worker never quits when employed in the most favorable contract represented by $W_0 = \overline{W}$, that contract smooths the worker's income by offering a wage that does not vary with tenure. Furthermore, the contract yields a positive expected profit under assumption A3.

Property 1. Given any initial value $W_0 \geq \overline{W} > U$ and wage w_0 defined by $u(w_0) = (\rho + \delta)W_0 - \delta U$, the stationary contract $w(t) = w_0$ is optimal. Furthermore, for $W_0 = \overline{W}$, $w_0 = \overline{w}$ and $\Pi(\overline{W}) = (p - \overline{w})/(r + \delta) > 0$.

Second, the optimal wage-tenure path is chosen to balance the employer's value of the reduction in the worker's incentive to quit associated with a rising wage with the cost of the reduction in consumption smoothing that the increase implies. The result is an increasing wage-tenure schedule if the value density is positive.

Property 2. Given $W \in [\underline{W}, \overline{W})$ and $W \geq U$, an optimal wage-tenure contract satisfies

$$\frac{-u''(w)}{u'(w)} \frac{dw}{dt} = \lambda F'(W) J u'(w). \tag{5.29}$$

The left side of the equation, the product of the risk aversion coefficient and the difference between tomorrow's and today's wage, is the utility cost to the worker of a small transfer of wage income from today to tomorrow. An increase in tomorrow's wage increases the worker's continuation value W tomorrow by an amount $u'(w)$ and decreases the quit probability, $q(W) = \lambda[1 - F(W)]$, by $q'(W) = -\lambda F'(W)$. Hence, the right side is the saving in turnover cost to the employer expressed in utility terms attributable to a small transfer of wage income from today to tomorrow.

Interestingly, neither the employer's nor the worker's rate of time preference directly enters this marginal condition because both cost and benefit are contemporaneous in continuous time. Equation (5.29) also requires a rising wage-tenure profile if and only if an increase in tomorrow's wage relative to today's affects the probability of a quit. In other words, if the employer has no nearby competitor in the sense that no potential outside offer slightly larger than w exists, namely, $F'(W) = 0$, then a small transfer of wage income from today to tomorrow has no effect on the worker's likelihood of quitting tomorrow. Consequently, the wage paid is locally independent of tenure in this case.

Property 2 implies that any optimal contract associated with an initial value to the worker less than the maximum available together with its associated continuation values to the worker is a particular solution to the ordinary autonomous differential equation system composed of equations (5.25), (5.27), and (5.29). Furthermore, Property 1 implies that the associated optimal wage paid is tenure invariant as is the associated continuation values to both parties at $W_0 = \overline{W}$. Indeed, these values $(\overline{w}, \overline{W}, \overline{J})$, defined by

$$u(\overline{w}) = (\rho + \delta)\overline{W} - \delta U \quad \text{and} \quad \overline{J} = \Pi(\overline{W}) = (p - \overline{w})/(r + \delta), \qquad (5.30)$$

represent the stationary solution to the differential equation system. Finally, the optimal wage paid at tenure t in every contract and the associated continuation values all converge to this stationary solution.

Property 3. If the contract $\overrightarrow{w}$ is optimal, then $\frac{dW(t, \overrightarrow{w})}{dt} > 0$ and $\lim_{t\to\infty}(w(t), W(t, \overrightarrow{w}), J(t, \overrightarrow{w})) = (\overline{w}, \overline{W}, \overline{J})$ for every fixed $\overline{W} > U$.

Collectively, the three properties provide the following characterization of an optimal wage-tenure contract.

Proposition 4. For any fixed c.d.f. $F(W)$ satisfying A2 and A3 and scalars $\overline{W}$ and U such that $\overline{W} > U$, the optimal contract and the sequences of continuation values associated with the initial contract value $W_0 \in [\underline{W}, \overline{W}]$ is the solution to the differential equation system

$$\frac{dw}{dt} = \left(\frac{-u'(w)^2}{u''(w)}\right)\lambda F'(W)J \qquad (5.31)$$

$$\frac{dW}{dt} = (\rho + \delta)W - u(w) - \delta U - \lambda \int_W^{\overline{W}} [x - W]\,dF(x) \qquad (5.32)$$

$$\frac{dJ}{dt} = (r + \delta + \lambda[1 - F(W)])\,J - (p - w) \qquad (5.33)$$

that satisfies $W(0) = W_0$ and $\lim_{t\to\infty}\{w(t), W(t), J(t)\} = (\overline{w}, \overline{W}, \overline{J})$, where $(\overline{w}, \overline{W}, \overline{J})$ is the stationary solution to the system.

Proof. See Burdett and Coles (2001).

In fact, $(\overline{w}, \overline{W}, \overline{J})$ is a stationary saddle point of the differential equation system and an optimal wage-tenure contract is the trajectory on the stable manifold converging to the stationary point determined by the initial value of the offer W_0. Note that as a corollary, Property 1 holds and any equilibrium offer density is zero at the highest wage, that is, $F'(\overline{W}) = 0$.

5.3.4 Labor Market Equilibrium

In this subsection, a labor market equilibrium distribution of contract values, $F(W)$, is characterized. Formally, it is a mixed strategy noncooperative solution to a wage-tenure contract offer game played by the employers in a market environment characterized by random matching and search friction. In the game, identical employers offer contracts to workers contacted at random in competition with all the other employers as in the Butters (1977) and the original Burdett-Mortensen model. The difference from the first of these models is that job-worker matches are long-lived and from the second is that the wage may differ with tenure.

The initial value to a worker of any particular wage-tenure contract, W_0, together with the distribution of workers over labor force states determines the probability that an applicant, viewed as a randomly chosen worker, will accept the offer. Given that any equilibrium offer must be acceptable to the unemployed in equilibrium and that workers only leave employers with contracts that offer a smaller continuation value,

$$h(W_0) = u + (1 - u)G(W_0), \tag{5.34}$$

where $G(W)$ is the fraction of employed workers with contract that have continuation value W or less. Of course, both u and $G(W)$ evolve over time in response to worker flows. Indeed, because all contracts offered in any equilibrium are acceptable, steady-state unemployment is

$$u = \frac{\delta}{\delta + \lambda}. \tag{5.35}$$

Similarly, because the flow of workers into employment under a contract of value W or less is the flow of unemployed workers contacted by firms with initial value W or less, $\lambda F(W)u$, and the outflow into this employment state is the flow of worker in the state who are either laid off or who quit to accept a more valuable contract offered by some alternative employer, $(\delta + \lambda[1 - F(W)])G(W)(1 - u)$, the fraction of employed workers with contracts that have continuation value W or less is

$$G(W) = \frac{\lambda F(W)u}{(\delta + \lambda[1 - F(w)])(1 - u)} = \frac{\delta F(W)}{\delta + \lambda[1 - F(W)]} \tag{5.36}$$

in steady state.

The expected profit per worker contacted given that the employer's contract offers the value W_0 is the product of the acceptance probability and the value of a filled job

$$\pi(W_0) = h(W_0)\Pi(W_0) \tag{5.37}$$

where $\Pi(W_0)$ is the maximal expected value of future profit attributable to a contract of initial value W_0 to the worker, as defined by equation (5.28). The noncooperative Nash equilibrium condition for an optimal contract choice by the firm and the characterization of an optimal contract in Theorem 1 have three implications. First, because all workers accept the most generous contract and no worker quits an employer offering that contract, expected profit per worker contact is given by

$$h(\overline{W})\Pi(\overline{W}) = \overline{J} = \frac{p - \overline{w}}{r + \delta}. \tag{5.38}$$

Second, the equilibrium distribution of offers, $F(W)$, is such that all contracts offered yield the same maximum expected profit per worker contacted, namely,

$$h(W_0)\Pi(W_0) \begin{cases} = \overline{J} & \text{for all } W_0 \in [\underline{W}, \overline{W}] \\ \leq \overline{J} & \text{otherwise} \end{cases}. \tag{5.39}$$

Finally, because only unemployed workers accept the least generous contract, its value to any worker is the value of unemployment:

$$\underline{W} = U. \tag{5.40}$$

Following Coles and Burdett, call the least generous contract, that determined by $W_0 = \underline{W} = U$, the baseline salary scale, and denote it as $\overrightarrow{w}^s$ and its continuation value as $W^s(t) = W(t, \overrightarrow{w}^s)$. As a corollary of Properties 2 and 3, we know that the pair of functions $(w^s(t), W^s(t))$ is increasing in t and converges to $(\overline{w}, \overline{W})$ as $t \to \infty$. Hence, given any $W_0 \in [\underline{W}, \overline{W}]$, a unique tenure value on the baseline contract t_0 exists such that $W_0 = W^s(t_0)$. Furthermore, as a consequence of the saddle path property of the collection of optimal contracts, the optimal contract defined by W_0 is the remainder of the baseline contract. This fact implies that the optimal contract given initial value W_0 is $w^*(t; W_0) = w^s(t+t_0)$. In other words, given the starting salary point t_0 defined by $W_0 = W^s(t_0)$, the optimal wage contract pays a worker with tenure t a wage commensurate with the tenure $t_0 + t$ on the baseline wage scale. Note that this fact also implies that firm's continuation payoff of the contract is $J^*(t, W_0) = J^s(t + t_0)$.

As a consequence, a worker quits to take another job offering W_0 if and only if the starting point on the corresponding wage scale (w_0, t_0) exceeds the point (w, t) on the baseline salary scale represented by the worker's current wage and tenure pair, namely, $W_0 = W^s(t_0) > W = W^s(t) \Leftrightarrow (w_0, t_0) > (w, t)$. Rather than regarding firms as competing by offering a contract value W_0, it is equivalent to take the view that each offers an alternative initial starting point t_0 on the baseline salary scale. The least generous offer defined by $W_0 = \underline{W}$ sets $t_0 = 0$ and then pays $w(t) = w^s(t)$ at higher tenures, while any other offer $W_0 > \underline{W}$ starts at $t_0 > 0$ and subsequently pays $w(t) = w^s(t + t_0)$.

Given this insight, define $F^s(t)$, $t \in [0, \infty)$ as the distribution of starting points on the baseline salary scale. Since $W_0 = W^s(t_0)$, one can define the probability that an offer starts at t or less on the baseline salary scale as

$$F^s(t) = F(W^s(t)). \tag{5.41}$$

The equal profit condition implies that this function is also a solution to a differential equation. Namely, because $\Pi(W^s(t)) = J(t, \overrightarrow{w}^s) = J^s(t)$ for all starting points, the equal profit condition (5.39) requires

$$\pi(W^s(t)) = h(W^s(t))J^s(t) = \overline{J} = \frac{p - \overline{w}}{r + \delta} \quad \forall t \in [0, \infty). \tag{5.42}$$

By differentiating (5.42) with respect to t, one obtains

$$J^s(t)h'(W^s(t))\frac{dW^s}{dt} + h(W^s(t))\frac{dJ^s(t)}{dt} = 0.$$

In other words, the positive effect of a more generous contract offer, a higher starting point t, on the acceptance probability is just off set by a corresponding decline in the initial continuation value of the match.

Equations (5.34), (5.27), (5.41), and (5.42) imply that

$$0 = J^s(t)h(W^s(t))\left(\frac{\lambda F'(W^s(t))\frac{dW^s}{dt}}{\delta + \lambda[1 - F(W^s(t))]}\right)$$

$$+ h(W^s(t))[(r + \delta + \lambda[1 - F^s(t)])J^s(t) - (p - w^s(t))]$$

$$= \left(\frac{\lambda\frac{dF^s}{dt}}{\delta + \lambda[1 - F^s(t)]}\right)\left(\frac{p - \overline{w}}{r + \delta}\right) + (r + \delta + \lambda[1 - F^s(t)])\left(\frac{p - \overline{w}}{r + \delta}\right)$$

$$- \frac{\delta(p - w^s)}{\delta + \lambda[1 - F^s(t)]}.$$

That is, $F^s(t)$ solves

$$\frac{dF^s}{dt} = \frac{\delta(r+\delta)}{\lambda}\left(\frac{p-w^s}{p-\overline{w}} - \frac{(\delta+\lambda[1-F^s(t)])(r+\delta+\lambda[1-F^s(t)])}{\delta(r+\delta)}\right).$$

$$(5.43)$$

Note that $\lim_{t\to\infty}\{dF^s/dt\} \to 0$ because $\lim_{t\to\infty}\{F^s(t)\} \to 1$ along the baseline contract.

To compute a solution to (5.43) one needs to know the baseline salary scale, the function $w^s(t)$ defined on $[0, \infty)$. In turn, it is a solution to the differential equation system (5.31)–(5.33) given $F(W(t)) = F^s(t)$. Following Burdett and Coles (2001), call the solution to the combined system of differential equations given $\underline{w}$ and U a *replication*. Then, a replication is a solution to the ODE system composed of equation (5.43) and

$$\frac{dW^s}{dt} = (\rho+\delta)W^s - u(w^s) - \delta U - \lambda S^s \tag{5.44}$$

$$\frac{dS^s}{dt} = -[1-F^s]\frac{dW^s}{dt} = -(1-F^s)[(\rho+\delta)W^s - u(w^s) - \delta U - \lambda S^s] \tag{5.45}$$

$$\frac{dw^s}{dt} = \left(\frac{-u'(w^s)^2}{u''(w^s)}\right)\lambda J^s(t)F'(W^s(t))$$

$$= \left(\frac{-u'(w^s)^2}{u''(w^s)}\right)\left(\frac{\lambda}{h(W^s(t))}\right)\overline{J}F'(W^s(t))$$

$$= \left(\frac{-u'(w^s)^2}{u''(w^s)}\right)\left(\frac{\lambda(p-\overline{w})(\delta+\lambda[1-F^s])}{\delta(r+\delta)}\right)\frac{\frac{dF^s}{dt}}{\frac{dW^s}{dt}}$$

$$= \left(\frac{-u'(w^s)^2(p-\overline{w})(\delta+\lambda[1-F^s])}{u''(w^s)}\right)$$

$$\times \left(\frac{\frac{p-w^s}{p-\overline{w}} - \frac{(\delta+\lambda[1-F^s(t)])(r+\delta+\lambda[1-F^s(t)])}{\delta(r+\delta)}}{(\rho+\delta)W^s - u(w^s) - \delta U - \lambda S^s}\right) \tag{5.46}$$

from equations (5.41) and (5.42), where

$$S^s(t) \equiv \int_{W^s(t)}^{\overline{W}}[x - W^s(t)]dF(x) \tag{5.47}$$

is the expected gain in value attributable to receiving an offer indexed by the starting value t on the baseline salary scale. Given $\underline{W}$ and U, Proposition 3, the definition of $S^s(t)$ and the requirement that $F^s(t)$ is a distribution function on $[0, t)$ imply that the limit of the solution of interest is the stationary point of the system, that is,

$$\lim_{t \to \infty} \{w^s(t), W^s(t), S^s(t), F^s(t)\} = (\overline{w}, \overline{W}, 0, 1). \tag{5.48}$$

Because this stationary solution is also a saddle point of the new ODE system, the unique solution is the segment of the stable manifold converging to it as t tends to infinity. Finally, the corresponding contract offer density can be constructed from a replication by using the definition (5.41).

Let $F^s(t) = F^s(t; U, \overline{W})$, $W^s(t) = W^s(t; U, \overline{W})$, and so forth represent the replication associated with any fixed pair of numbers $(U, \overline{W})$ representing the support of the distribution of contract offers $F(W)$. The equilibrium values of unemployment and the largest contract value solve

$$U = \underline{W} = W^s(0; U, \overline{W}) \tag{5.49}$$

and

$$\rho U = u(b) + \lambda S^s(0; U, \overline{W}) \tag{5.50}$$

from equation (5.40) and (5.26). A *labor market equilibrium*, then, is a replication that satisfies these two boundary conditions and yields nonnegative profit, namely,

$$\overline{J} = \frac{p - \overline{w}}{r + \delta} \geq 0.$$

Proposition 5. A labor market equilibrium solution exists that satisfies A1, A2, and A3 if and only if $p > b$.

Proof. See Burdett and Coles (2001).

5.4 Summary

In this chapter, the basic Burdett-Mortensen model is extended to allow for more flexible wage policies. Two approaches are studied. In the first, employers match outside offers while, in the second, employers offer wage-tenure contracts. Although the two approaches appear to be quite different, they actually have similar implications. Namely, the two models provide still another explanation for why wages rise with tenure on a job. However, because workers do not become more productive with tenure, both models also suggest that the positive wage-tenure relations reflect intrafirm wage dispersion.

Postel-Vinay and Robin (1999, 2001) assume that an employer pays each worker his reservation wage initially and then matches outside options as they are generated in the future when doing so is optimal from the employer's perspective. Stevens (1999) and Burdett and Coles (2001) continue to assume that employers precommit to a wage contract but these contracts allow the wage to depend on the worker's job tenure. In both cases, the wage earned by a worker rises with experience on average for the same reason it does in the original Burdett-Mortensen model. Those with longer spells of employment are more likely to be found higher on the "job ladder." Wages rise with tenure in the Postel-Vinay–Robin model because workers are generally paid less than their value of marginal product and, consequently, their employer is willing to match some outside offers. Although employers do not match outside offers in the Burdett-Coles model, they do find it optimal to offer "back loaded" wage-tenure schedules to discourage employee searches for a higher wage.

Both approaches are alternative forms of a "discriminating monopsonist" formulation of wage determination. Indeed, employers expropriate all the match rents, at least in the case of risk-neutral workers assumed by Postel-Vinay and Robin and by Stevens. Given risk aversion as assumed by Burdett and Coles, the only equilibrium is one in which different employers offer different contracts as in the original Burdett-Mortensen formulation. Hence, those unemployed workers who are lucky enough to find the better offers realize match rents.

The two alternative wage determination formulations also raise several research questions of interest. The Burdett-Coles model currently does not allow for employer heterogeneity. Would workers take a wage cut to move to a more productive firm in a generalized version of their model? Would the wage-tenure schedule of more productive employer rise more steeply? I conjecture that these stochastic properties of the Postel-Vinay–Robin model would carry over, but I do not have a convincing proof.

What are the comparative welfare implications of the two formulations? Although it is true that in the Postel-Vinay–Robin model separations are efficient from the point of view of any existing worker-employer pair, it does not follow that their solution is socially more efficient than the solution to the Burdett-Coles model for at least two reasons. First, the employer strategy of matching outside offers generally encourages too much worker search on the job when an intensity decision is allowed. Second, matching offers does not provide income smoothing of the kind that would benefit risk-averse employees. Hence, even if one ignores the fact that the sequential auction formulation of the wage dispersion requires perfect and symmetric information about offer terms, the fixed contract equilibrium may have superior welfare properties. Indeed, it could be that employers are better off ex post in the Burdett-Coles equilibrium even if the information required to implement the Postel-Vinay–Robin equilibrium were not an issue. More study of this question should provide insight into why most markets are not like that for academic economists in the United States.

Notes

1. See Farber (1999) for a recent review of the debate.

2. In their latest paper, Postel-Vinay and Robin (2002) consider this possibility. Their initial results suggest that it is the least productive who have an incentive to commit to a no response policy while the more productive employers find it more profitable to match outside offers.

3. As in the case of the papers under study as well as the original Burdett-Mortensen model, I abstract from a search intensity choice in this chapter.

4. The inequality accounts for the fact that some employed worker may prefer the deviation to a fixed wage if the wage earned is low enough.

5. The authors also show that their results apply in the case of more general worker preferences—namely, that workers maximize the expect present value of the utility of the future wage stream where the instantaneous utility function is any in the CARA family.

Appendix: An Existence Proof

For the reasons cited, the lower support of both the wage and productivity distribution is the reservation wage $R = b$ given free entry by equation (4.20). Interpret $\phi : [b, \overline{p}] \to \mathbb{R}_+$ as the flow of contacts made by firms of productivity p or more. Then, for any strictly increasing wage policy function $w(p)$,

$$\lambda[1 - F(w(p))] = m \int_p^{\overline{p}} v(x, w(x)) \, d\Gamma(x) = \phi(p) \qquad \text{(A.1)}$$

from equations (4.21) and (4.22). Let the search intensity of worker employed by a firm of type p be represented as

$$\sigma(p) = s(w(p)). \qquad \text{(A.2)}$$

As the necessary and sufficient first-order condition for an optimal search effort choice implied by (4.6) is

$$c'_w(s(w)) = \int_w^{\overline{w}} \left(\frac{\lambda[1 - F(x)]}{r + \delta + \lambda s(x)[1 - F(x)]} \right) dx$$

by Assumption 3, $\sigma(p)$ can be regarded as the solution to the following equivalent differential equation:

$$c''_w(\sigma)\sigma' + \frac{\phi w'}{r + \delta + \sigma\phi} = 0, \qquad \text{(A.3)}$$

where $\sigma(\overline{p}) = 0$ is the required boundary condition. The definition (A.1) implies

$$\phi' + v\Gamma'(p) = 0, \qquad \text{(A.4)}$$

where $\phi(\overline{p}) = 0$ is the boundary condition, and

$$v(p) = v(p, w(p)) \tag{A.5}$$

represents the optimal recruiting effort of a productivity p type firm. Equations (A.3) and (A.4) are two differential equations common to the system characterizing market equilibrium given either wage determination model.

A.1 Monopsony Model

In the case of monopsony, the necessary first-order condition for an optimal wage choice, one that satisfies (4.18), can be written as

$$\frac{h'(w)}{h(w)} - \frac{d'(w)}{r + d(w)} - \frac{1}{p - w} = 0. \tag{A.6}$$

Because the steady-state condition (4.11) implies

$$\frac{G'(w)}{\delta + \lambda \int_w^{\overline{w}} s(x)\,dG(x)} = \frac{F'(w)}{\delta + \lambda s(w)[1 - F(w)]},$$

a differentiation of equations (4.12) and (4.13) respectively yields

$$\frac{h'(w)}{h(w)} = \frac{\lambda s(w)G'(w)}{\delta + \lambda \int_w^{\overline{w}} s(x)\,dG(x)} = \frac{\lambda s(w)F'(w)}{\delta + \lambda s(w)[1 - F(w)]} \tag{A.7}$$

and

$$\frac{d'(w)}{r + d(w)} = \frac{\lambda s'(w)[1 - F(w)] - \lambda s(w)F'(w)}{r + \delta + \lambda s(w)[1 - F(w)]}.$$

These equations collectively imply the following differential equation representation of the wage policy function:

$$\frac{w'}{p - w} + \frac{\phi\sigma'}{r + \delta + \sigma\phi} + \frac{[r + 2(\delta + \sigma\phi)]\sigma\phi'}{(r + \delta + \sigma\phi)(\delta + \sigma\phi)} = 0, \tag{A.8}$$

where $w(b) = b$.

The recruiting effort of a firm characterized by p solves

$$c'_f(v(p)) = \frac{h(w(p))(p - w(p))}{r + d(w(p))} \tag{A.9}$$

from (4.17) and Assumption 4. As $w(p)$ maximizes the right-hand side in the monopsony case, the differential equation

$$\frac{c_f''(v)v'}{c_f'(v)} = \frac{1}{p-w}, \tag{A.10}$$

where $v(b) = 0$ represents $v(p)$, the contact frequency of a firm of productivity type p. Now, equations (A.3), (A.4), (A.8), and (A.10) form a system of first-order differential equations and boundary conditions that uniquely determine the equilibrium wage policy function $w(p)$ for monopsony and the related offer arrival frequency, search effort, and recruiting effort functions $\phi(p)$, $\sigma(p)$, and $v(p)$ on the support of the given productivity distribution.

A.2 Bilateral Bargaining Model

In the generalized Nash bargaining case, the necessary and sufficient first-order condition for a solution to (4.19) can be written as

$$\beta\left(\frac{W'(w)}{W(w)-U}\right) - (1-\beta)\left(\frac{d'(w)}{r+d(w)} + \frac{1}{p-w}\right) = 0. \tag{A.11}$$

Letting

$$\omega(p) = W(w(p)) - U \tag{A.12}$$

represent the surplus value to a worker of employment in a firm of type p, it follows that

$$\omega' = \frac{w'}{r+\delta+\sigma\phi}, \tag{A.13}$$

where $\omega(b) = 0$ from (4.4), (A.1), and (A.2). Finally, after multiplying all the terms in (A.11) by w', one obtains the differential equation

$$\frac{w'}{p-w} + \frac{\phi\sigma'}{r+\delta+\sigma\phi} + \frac{\sigma\phi'}{r+\delta+\sigma\phi} = \frac{\beta}{1-\beta}\frac{\omega'}{\omega}, \quad \text{where } w(b) = b \tag{A.14}$$

after appropriate substitution. In this case, equations (A.1), (A.2), (A.7),

(A.9), (A.11), and (A.12) imply

$$\frac{c''(v)}{c'(v)}v' = \left(\frac{h'(w)}{h(w)} - \frac{d'(w)}{r+d(w)} - \frac{1}{p-w}\right)w'(p) + \frac{1}{p-w}$$

$$= \left(\frac{h'(w)}{h(w)} - \left(\frac{\beta}{1-\beta}\right)\frac{W'(w)}{W(w)-U}\right)w'(p) + \frac{1}{p-w}$$

$$= \frac{\lambda s(w)F'(w)w'(p)}{\delta + \lambda s(w)[1-F(w)]} - \left(\frac{\beta}{1-\beta}\right)\frac{W'(w)w'(p)}{W(w)-U} + \frac{1}{p-w}.$$

Therefore,

$$\frac{c''(v)}{c'(v)}v' + \frac{\sigma\phi'}{\delta+\sigma\phi} + \frac{\beta\omega'}{(1-\beta)\omega} = \frac{1}{p-w}, \tag{A.15}$$

where $v(b) = 0$. Hence, equations (A.3), (A.13), (A.14), (A.15), and (A.4) form a system of first-order differential equations and boundary conditions that uniquely determine the equilibrium wage policy function $w(p)$ in the bilateral bargaining case and the related functions $\phi(p)$, $\sigma(p)$, $v(p)$, and $\omega(p)$ defined on the support of the given productivity distribution.

Afterword

Why are similar workers paid differently? Why do some jobs pay more than others? I have argued that wage dispersion of this kind reflects differences in employer productivity. More productive employers offer higher pay to attract and retain more workers. Workers flow from less to more productive employers in response to these pay differences, and both workers and employers invest search and recruiting efforts in that reallocation process. Exogenous turnover and job destruction on the one hand, and search friction on the other, prevent the labor market from ever attaining a state in which all workers are employed by the most productive firms. Instead, a continuous process of reallocation of workers from less to more productive employers interrupted by transitions to nonemployment induced by job destruction and other reasons for labor turnover generates a steady-state allocation of labor across firms of differing productivity. Of course, the assertion that wage dispersion is the consequence of productivity dispersion begs another question: What is the explanation for productivity dispersion? Although an extensive and convincing answer to the question is the topic for another book, some speculation is in order here.

As I have emphasized, search and recruiting friction supports persistent productivity dispersion. Arbitrage alone on either side of the labor market cannot weed out inefficient firms. Because of the option to search on the job, unemployed workers accept low wages and poor working conditions for the time required to find a better job. On the employer's side of the market, the most efficient few among employers find it profitable to limit their size in the face of recruiting and hiring costs that rise at the margin and of exogenous turnover. Hence, any source of wage dispersion persists.

One of the insights of the Burdett-Mortensen approach is that the strategic wage setting forces can generate both wage and productivity dispersion without any other external cause. Even if this source of dispersion is insufficient, however, one would expect that the option to invest in both general and specific capital should amplify any exogenous differences in labor productivity across employers. More empirical work on this idea, along the lines pioneered by Rosholm and Svarer (2000), is needed. The nature of job flow data constructed by Davis, Haltiwanger, and Schuh (1996) for the United States and recently replicated for many countries including Denmark (see Albaek and Sorensen 1998) provide strong support for the view that individual firms experience persistent idiosyncratic productivity shocks. As Davis, Haltiwanger, and Schuh document, employment growth at the firm level is best described by a distribution with a broad support on both sides of zero. Although across-firm dispersion in job growth is a fact of life, a firm's location in the distribution typically reflects its own life cycle. In every industry and region, new firms are being born, some are expanding, others contracting, and a few are dying. The dynamic processes that support these facts seem to be good candidates for the kinds of exogenous productivity dispersion needed to explain firm-level wage differences. But what are these processes?

Relative demand and productive efficiency of individual firms are continually shocked by events. The shocks are the consequence of changes in tastes, changes in regulations, and changes induced by globalization among others. Another important source of persistent productivity differences across firms is the process of adopting technical innovation. We know that the diffusion of new and more efficient methods is a slow, drawn-out affair. Experimentation is required to implement new methods. Many innovations are embodied in equipment and forms of human capital that are necessarily long-lived. Learning how and where to apply any new innovation takes time and may well be highly firm specific. Since old technologies are not immediately replaced by the new for all of these reasons, productive efficiency varies considerably across firms at any point in time.

Finally, the fact that within-skill-category wage dispersion has increased as much as the returns to education in the United States is suggestive. It may well be that recent innovations in computer- and communications-based technologies have been skill biased. It may also be that the productivity of every skill category is higher in those firms who are the leaders in the application of these technologies. If so, we should see a diminishing of within-skill-category wage dispersion in the longer run both as workers are reallocated from the less to the more efficient firms over time by the processes described in this book and as the shocks generated by the computer revolution diminish in amplitude and frequency.

These are a few of the possible sources of productivity dispersion that could be at the root of differences one sees in pay policy across firms. Coming to a better understanding of these processes is important for explaining the differences in the wages for similar workers.

Bibliography

Note: Sources listed in the bibliography are not necessarily cited in the text.

Abowd, J. M., and F. Kramarz. 1999. "The Analysis of Labor Markets Using Matched Employer-Employee Data." Chap. 26 in O. Ashenfelter and D. Card, eds., *Handbook of Labor Economics* 3(B), 2629–2710. Amsterdam: North-Holland.

Abowd, J., and F. Kramarz. 2000a. "Inter-industry and Firm-size Wage Differentials in the United States." Cornell University working paper.

Abowd, J., and F. Kramarz. 2000b. "The Structure of Compensation in France and in the United States." Cornell University working paper.

Abowd, J. M., R. H. Creecy, and F. Kramarz. 2002. "Computing Person and Firm Effects Using Linked Longitudinal Employer-Employee Data." Cornell University working paper.

Abowd, J. M., H. Finer, and F. Kramarz. 1999. "Individual and Firm Heterogeneity in Compensation." In J. C. Haltiwanger, J. I. Lane, J. R. Spletzer, J. Theeuwes, eds., *The Creation and Analysis of Employer-Employee Matched Data.* Amsterdam: North-Holland.

Abowd, J. M., F. Kramarz, and D. Margolis. 1999. "High Wage Workers and High Wage Firms." *Econometrica* 67: 251–334.

Acemoglu, D., and R. Shimer. 1999. "Wage and Technology Dispersion." *Review of Economic Studies* 68: 585–608.

Albaek, K., and E. S. Madsen. 1996. "Plant-size Wage Effects in Denmark." Mimeo., University of Copenhagen.

Albaek, K., and B. E. Sorensen. 1998. "Worker and Job Flows in Danish Manufacturing." *Economic Journal* 108: 1750–1771.

Albaek, K., M. Arai, R. Asplund, E. Barth, and E. S. Madsen. 1996. "Employer Size-Wage Effects in the Nordic Countries." *Economic Journal* 5: 525–448.

Albrecht, J. W., and B. Axell. 1984. "An Equilibrium Model of Search Unemployment." *Journal of Political Economy* 92: 824–840.

Altonji, J., and R. Shakotko. 1985. "Do Wages Rise with Seniority?" *Review of Economic Studies* 54: 437–459.

Albrecht, J., and B. Axell. 1984. "An Equilibrium Model of Search Unemployment." *Journal of Political Economy* 92: 824–840.

Becker, G. 1973. "A Theory of Marriage, Part 1." *Journal of Political Economy* 81: 813–846.

Bontemps, C., J.-M. Robin, and G. J. van den Berg. 1999. "An Empirical Equilibrium Job Search Model with Search on the Job and Heterogenous Workers." *International Economic Review* 40: 1039–1075.

Bontemps, C., J.-M. Robin, and G. J. van den Berg. 2000. "Equilibrium Search with Continuous Productivity Dispersion: Theory and Non-Parameteric Estimation. *International Economic Review* 41: 305–358.

Bowlus, A. J., N. M. Kiefer, and G. R. Neumann. 1995. "Estimation of Equilibrium Wage Distributions with Heterogeneity." *Journal of Applied Econometrics* 10: S119–S131.

Bronfenbrenner, M. 1956. "Potential Monopsony in the Labor Market." *Industrial and Labor Relations Review* 9: 577–588.

Brown, C., and J. L. Medoff. 1989. "The Employer Size-Wage Effect." *Journal of Political Economy* 97: 1027–1059.

Bulow, J., and L. Summers. 1986. "A Theory of Dual Labor Markets with Applications to Industrial Policy, Discrimination, and Keynesian Unemployment." *Journal of Labor Economics* 4: 376–414.

Bunzel, H., B. J. Christensen, P. Jensen, N. Kiefer, L. Korsholm, L. Muus, G. Neumann, and M. Rosholm. 2000. "Specification and Estimation of Equilibrium Search Models." In H. Bunzel et al., eds., *Panel Data and Structural Labor Market Models*. Amsterdam: Elsevier.

Burdett, K. 1978. "Employee Search and Quits." *American Economic Review* 68: 212–220.

Burdett, K., and M. G. Coles. 2001. "Wage Tenure Contracts and Equilibrium Search." Mimeo., University of Essex.

Burdett, K., and K. Judd. 1983. "Equilibrium Price Dispersion." *Econometrica* 51: 955–970.

Burdett, K., and D. T. Mortensen. 1998. "Wage Differentials, Employer Size, and Unemployment." *International Economic Review* 39: 257–273.

Butters, G. R. 1977. "Equilibrium Distributions of Sales and Advertising Prices." *Review of Economic Studies* 44: 465–491.

Card, D., and A. B. Kruger. 1995. *Myth and Measurement*. Princeton: Princeton University Press.

Christensen, B. J., R. Lentz, D. T. Mortensen, G. R. Neumann, and A. Werwatz. 2001. "On the Job Search and the Wage Distribution." Northwestern University working paper.

Coles, M. G. 2001. "Equilibrium Wage Dispersion, Firm Size and Growth." *Review of Economic Dynamics* 4: 159–187.

Davis, S. J., and J. C. Haltiwanger. 1991. "Wage Dispersion within and between Manufacturing Plants." *Brookings Papers on Economic Activity: Microeconomics,* 115–180.

Davis, S. J., and J. C. Haltiwanger. 1996. "Employer Size and the Wage Structure in U.S. Manufacturing." *Annales D'Economie et de Statistique* (June): 323–368.

Davis, S. J., J. C. Haltiwanger, and S. Schuh. 1996. *Job Creation and Destruction*. Cambridge, MA: The MIT Press.

Diamond, P. A. 1971. "A Model of Price Adjustment." *Journal of Economic Theory* 3: 156–168.

Diamond, P. A. 1982. "Wage Determination and Efficiency in Search Equilibrium." *Review of Economic Studies* 49: 217–227.

Dickens, W. T., and L. Katz. 1987. "Inter-Industry Wage Differences and Industry Characteristics." In K. Land and J. S. Leonard, eds., *Unemployment and the Structure of the Labor Market.* Oxford: Blackwell.

Doms, M., T. Dunne, and K. R. Troske. 1997. "Workers, Wages, and Technology." *Quarterly Journal of Economics* 112: 252–290.

Due, J., J. S. Madsen, C. S. Jensen, and L. K. Petersen. 1994. *The Survival of the Danish Model.* Copenhagen: DJØF Publishing.

Eckstein, Z., and K. I. Wolpin. 1990. "Estimating a Market Equilibrium Search Model from Panel Data on Individuals." *Econometrica* 58: 783–808.

Farber, H. 1999. "Mobility and Stability: The Dynamics of Job Change in Labor Markets." In O. Ashenfelter and D. Card, eds., *Handbook of Labor Economics,* vol. 3B, 2440–2483. Amsterdam: Elsevier Science.

Frederiksen, A., and N. Westergard-Nielsen. 2002. "Where Did They Go?" Working paper, Aarhus School of Business.

Galenson, W. 1952. *The Danish System of Labor Relations: A Study in Industrial Peace.* Cambridge: Harvard University Press.

Gibbons, R., and L. Katz. 1992. "Does Unmeasured Ability Explain Inter-Industry Wage Differentials?" *Review of Economic Studies* 59: 515–535.

Haltiwanger, J. C., J. I. Lane, and J. R. Spletzer. 2000. "Wage, Productivity, and the Dynamic Interaction of Businesses and Workers." NBER Working Paper 7994.

Hamermesh, D. S. 1993. *Labor Demand.* Princeton: Princeton University Press.

Hwang, H., D. T. Mortensen, and W. R. Reed. 1998. "Hedonic Wages and Labor Market Search." *Journal of Labor Economics* 16: 815–847.

Katz, L. F., and D. H. Autor. 1999. "Changes in the Wage Structure and Earnings Inequality." In O. Ashenfelter and D. Card, eds., *Handbook of Labor Economics,* vol. 3A, 1463–1548. Amsterdam: Elsevier Science.

Katz, L. F., and K. M. Murphy. 1992. "Changes in Relative Wages, 1963–1987: Supply and Demand Factors." *Quarterly Journal of Economics:* 35–78.

Koning, P., G. J. van den Berg, G. Ridder, and K. Albaek. 2000. "The Relation Between Wages and Labor Market Frictions: An Empirical Analysis Based on Worker-Firm Data." In H. Bunzel, B. J. Christensen, P. Jensen, N. M. Kiefer, and D. T. Mortensen, eds., *Panel Data and Structural Labour Market Models.* Amsterdam: Elsevier.

Krueger, A. B., and L. H. Summers. 1988. "Efficiency Wages and the Inter-Industry Wage Structure." *Econometrica* 56: 259–294.

Lang, K., and S. Majumdar. 1999. "The Pricing of Job Characteristics When Markets Do Not Clear: Theory and Policy Implications." Department of Economics, Boston University.

Manning, A. 2001. *Monopsony in Motion*. Manuscript. Forthcoming from Princeton University Press.

Mortensen, D. T. 1970. "A Theory of Wage and Employment Dynamics." In E. S. Phelps, ed., *Microeconomic Foundations of Employment and Inflation Theory*, 124–166. New York: W. W. Norton.

Mortensen, D. T. 1982. "The Matching Process as a Noncooooperative/Bargaining Game." In J. J. McCall, ed., *The Economics of Information and Uncertainty*, 233–254. Chicago: University of Chicago Press.

Mortensen, D. T. 1990. "Equilibrium Wage Distributions: A Synthesis." In J. Hartog, G. Ridder, and J. Theeuwes, eds., *Panel Data and Labor Market Studies*. Amsterdam: North-Holland.

Mortensen, D. T. 2000. "Equilibrium Unemployment with Wage Posting: Burdett-Mortensen Meet Pissarides." In H. Bunzel, B. J. Christensen, P. Jensen, N. M. Kiefer, and D. T. Mortensen, eds., *Panel Data and Structural Labour Market Model*. Amsterdam: Elsevier.

Mortensen, D. T., and C. A. Pissarides. 1994. "Job Creation and Job Destruction in the Theory of Unemployment." *Review of Economic Studies* 61: 397–415.

Mortensen, D. T., and C. A. Pissarides. 1999a. "Job Reallocation and Employment Fluctuations." In M. Woodford and J. B. Taylor, eds., *Handbook of Macro Economics*, vol. 1B, 1171–1227. Amsterdam: Elsevier Science.

Mortensen, D. T., and C. A. Pissarides. 1999b. "New Developments in Models of Search in the Labor Market." In O. Ashenfelter and D. Card, eds., *Handbook of Labor Economics*, vol. 3B, 2567–2624. Amsterdam: Elsevier Science.

Murphy, K. M., and R. Topel. 1987. "Unemployment, Risk, and Earnings: Testing for Equalizing Wage Differences in the Labor Market." In K. Land and J. S. Leonard, eds., *Unemployment and the Structure of the Labor Market*. Oxford: Blackwell.

Murphy, K. M., and R. Topel. 1990. "Efficiency Wages Reconsidered: Theory and Evidence." In Y. Weiss and G. Fishelson, eds., *Advances in the Theory and Measurement of Unemployment*, 204–240. New York: St. Martin's Press.

Neal, D., and S. Rosen. 2000. "Theories of the Distribution of Earning." In A. B. Atkinson and F. Bourguignon, eds., *Handbook of Income Distribution, Volume 1*. Amsterdam: Elsevier Science B. V.

Oi, W. Y., and T. L. Idson. 1999. "Firm Size and Wages." In O. Ashenfelter and D. Card, eds., *Handbook of Labor Economics*, vol. 3B, 2165–2214. Amsterdam: Elsevier.

Phelps, E. S. 1970. "Money Wage Dynamics and Market Equilibrium." In E. S. Phelps, ed., *Microeconomic Foundations of Employment and Inflation Theory*, 124–166. New York: W. W. Norton.

Pissarides, C. A. 1985. "Short-Run Equilibrium Dynamics of Unemployment, Vacancies and Real Wages." *American Economic Review* 75: 676–690.

Pissarides, C. A. 2000. *Equilibrium Unemployment Theory*. 2d ed. Cambridge, MA: The MIT Press.

Postel-Vinay, F., and J.-M. Robin. 1999. "The Distribution of Earnings in an Equilibrium Search Model with State-Dependent Offers and Counter-Offers." INRA-LEA working paper.

Postel-Vinay, F., and J.-M. Robin. 2001. "An Equilibrium Job Search Model for Matched Employer-Employee Data." INRA-LEA working paper. Forthcoming in *Econometrica*.

Postel-Vinay, F., and J.-M. Robin. 2002. "To Match or Not to Match? Optimal Wage Policy with Endogenous Worker Search Intensity." Working paper.

Rosholm, M., and M. Svarer. 2000. "Wage, Training, Turnover in a Search-Matching Model." IZA Discussion Paper no. 223.

Rothschild, M. 1973. "Models of Market Organization with Imperfect Information: A Survey." *Journal of Political Economy* 81: 1283–1308.

Roy, A. D. 1950. "The Distribution of Earnings and Individual Output." *Economic Journal* 60: 489–505.

Roy, A. D. 1951. "Some Thoughts on the Distribution of Earning." *Oxford Economic Papers* (New Series) 3: 135–146.

Samuelson, P. A. 1951. *Economics: An Introductory Analysis*. New York: McGraw-Hill.

Shapiro, C., and J. Stiglitz. 1984. "Equilibrium Unemployment as a Worker Discipline Device." *American Economic Review* 74: 433–444.

Shimer, R. 2001. "The Assignment of Workers to Jobs in an Economy with Coordination Friction." NBER Working Paper 8501.

Shimer, R., and L. Smith. 2000. "Assortative Matching and Search." *Econometrica* 68: 371–398.

Stevens, M. 1999. "Wage-Tenure Contraction in a Frictional Labour Market: Firms' Strategies for Recruitment and Retention." Mimeo.

Index